The Geography of Planning Decisions

JOHN M. HALL

Theory and Practice in Geography

OXFORD UNIVERSITY PRESS · 1982

Oxford University Press, Walton Street, Oxford OX2 6DP
London Glasgow New York Toronto
Delhi Bombay Calcutta Madras Karachi
Kuala Lumpur Singapore Hong Kong Tokyo
Nairobi Dar es Salaam Cape Town
Melbourne Auckland

and associate companies in
Beirut Berlin Ibadan Mexico City

Published in the United States by
Oxford University Press, New York

British Library Cataloguing in Publication Data
Hall, John M.
The geography of planning decisions.–(Theory and practice in geography)
1. Land–Great Britain 2. Regional planning–Great Britain
I. Title II. Series
333.73'0941 HD596
ISBN 0-19-874034-4

Library of Congress Cataloging in Publication Data
Hall, John M.
The geography of planning decisions.
(Theory and practice in geography)
1. Land use–Great Britain–Planning. I. Title
II. Series.
HD596.H29 333.5'068 81-16909
ISBN 0-19-874034-4 AACR2

Set by Hope Services, Abingdon
and Printed in Great Britain
by J. W. Arrowsmith Ltd. Bristol

Contents

1 Introduction

Land use planning is about people and politics in managed places. The continually changing distribution, numbers, and activity patterns of people within localities, regions, and the nation generate demands for new investment, or cause the abandonment of earlier investment, in what is now often called the 'built environment' and the interstitial countryside. Controversy about the desirable visible form and particular location of the investment is expressed in political debate–sometimes through local and central government institutions, sometimes through spontaneous local protest on non-party-political lines. And the outcome of public and private investment decisions–estimated recently in the order of £6,000m. a year in Britain (Eversley and Moody, 1976)–is that some places change rapidly in their perceived desirability and convenience. The visible is reinforced by the invisible: withholding investment, even foregoing necessary repairs, can convince other potential investors that an area is going downhill, so accelerating its decay. The rather metaphysical rhetoric is used intentionally, for planning in practice has much to do with beliefs and the art of persuasion.

This volume has been arranged to show how statutory planning is contributing to the changing geography of town and country in Britain. Planning is what planners do, of course, and its practitioners would appear especially prone to seduction by the swings of fashion in both philosophy and technique. A sharp philosophical shift became evident with the return of a Conservative government after the general election of 1979. Several MPs and ministers regard many aspects of physical land use planning as an irritating hindrance on individual freedom and on the operation of the market economy, and the Local Government, Planning and Land Act 1980 was framed, in part, to dismantle some of the accumulated intricacies of planning procedure.

Readers wishing more closely to follow legislation filtering through into working practices can be recommended to two British journals: *The Planner*, published six times a year by the Royal Town Planning Institute, 26 Portland Place, London W1N 4BN; and *Town and Country Planning*, the journal of the independent Town and Country Planning Association, 15 Carlton House Terrace, London SW1Y 5AS, published eleven times a year. The association also publishes the weekly *Planning Bulletin*–a summary of press items and a digest of the latest reports and plans. Other journals are cited among the detailed references beginning on page 58; most of the journals and books should be available in college and larger public libraries. Commission and committee reports appear under the chairman's name.

2 The planners and the planning system

The 10,000 or so people who work in a British local 'planning office' and bear or seek the letters MRTPI–Member of the Royal Town Planning Institute–after their name are only a small, albeit influential, group among those who are in fact 'the planners'. Anyone who seeks to arrange events in order to secure desired change in the future is a 'planner'. Planning is simply the application of forethought; the consideration of the most appropriate means of achieving desired ends in the future (for definitions see Faludi, 1973). In land use planning what was once the absolute prerogative of the rich and powerful–the land-owning church, gentry, and nobility–is now hedged about by customs and public laws, and indeed much land has now been acquired for public housing and institutional uses. As an increasingly heterogeneous professional group, the MRTPIs see one of their roles as the safeguarding of the mysteries of the craft, in part through approving training courses for planners.

Table 1 identifies the wider group of 'planners' and lists some of the major curbs placed on their actions in the evolution of planned landscapes–a phrase which I like to contract to 'plannedscapes'. As will become clear in this chapter and the next, anyone in England and Wales (for Scotland maintains a distinctive legal tradition) who wants to build, engineer, or mine 'in, on, over or under the land', or to alter materially the use of buildings, has to apply for 'planning permission' from the local 'planning authority'. The planning committee of the local council comprises elected politicians (councillors) and they are advised by a selected staff from the planning department (council officers) who, having regard to local financial and political circumstance, interpret the broad intention of national legislation and practice. One planning department, in the Metropolitan Borough of Trafford, Greater Manchester, states its purpose in the borough handbook as being 'to help make the Borough a better place in which to live. Its chief concern is with the environment; to ensure that it is pleasant, safe, healthy and convenient; that you can travel comfortably and quickly and that business can move its goods and materials without damaging the way we want to live.'

The phrase 'pleasant, safe, healthy and convenient' encapsulates the several strands of effort which have been absorbed into the syllabus of land use planning.

Amenity or *pleasantness* reminds us of the 'city beautiful' school of what might now be termed 'architect-planners' who reviled the industrial city and who sought verdure in the stead of ugliness. Practical

TABLE 1 *Considerations for the plannedscape makers*

The potential investors . . .

whether households, private firms, or public agencies and institutions, whose family circumstances, vulnerability in business cycles, or party political control can change at short notice . . .

. . . want to 'develop'

by constructing new buildings, adaptations and extensions, engineering operations, or changes of use of existing buildings, using surveying and design skills and the resources of the construction industry . . .

. . . at particular places

bearing in mind the costs imposed by the physical *site* conditions and advantages of the broader geographical *situation* which helps to determine the desirability and hence the economic value of the site . . .

. . . at a particular time

bearing in mind that their particular desires cannot be separated from the prevailing climate of *investment* in private and public money markets, the seeming arbitrariness of local and central government's *political predilections*, and even the anticipated changes of personal and corporate *taxation* . . .

. . . but have to satisfy the law

of *restrictive covenants* relating to the particular property, of locally enforced *building regulations*, and locally enforced but nationally applied *planning permission*, granted by a planning committee advised by planning officials who consider the local statutory development plan . . .

. . . and may even have to recognize

that there may be users (and even beholders) of their land and buildings–other than themselves–who have strong *views* about the form of proposed changes, for places and owners' actions are endowed with *emotional attributes*; so development proposals may be contested by discontented citizens and groups.

---

designs were often commissioned by philanthropic patrons such as Sir Titus Salt at Saltaire, West Yorkshire, Cadburys at Bournville, West Midlands, and Rowntrees at New Earswick, North Yorkshire (Bell and Bell, 1969). Pleasantness and tidiness were also coveted by the countryside movement, notably in the early campaigns of the Council for the Preservation (now 'Protection') of Rural England (MacEwan, 1976).

Safety calls to mind the early traffic engineers who in this century sought the segregation of vehicles and pedestrians–especially children on the way to and from school (examples are given in Tetlow and Goss, 1968).

The *public health* origins of controls over city form are most important: long before the term 'planners' was widespread (the Town Planning

Institute was formed in 1914) enlightened city administrators and outspoken reformers pressed for better sanitation, wholesome water, lower density housing layouts, adequate daylight and ventilation.

It was long thought that *convenience* was largely a matter of disposition–the right thing in the right place. Planners often realize now that the narrow bands of time which people use daily in getting to work, school, shops, and entertainment, and home again, often defy their best attempts to promote convenient access. And convenience is not shared equally: for many individuals their lack of mobility may make a nonsense of general claims about improved accessibility.

The growth of planning

Although in British towns the individual property owner has long been obliged to conform to local regulations, planning as a widespread activity dates only from the last half-century or so. Indeed effective national policy-making and administrative co-ordination dates only from the Second World War. Cherry (1974) gives a detailed analysis of the evolution of planning in its institutionalized form, and his peacetime history volume (1975) on the evolution of countryside policy and legislation is mirrored for land use planning by Cullingworth (1975, 1979); both authors used Cabinet Office material in compiling their official histories. This chapter now outlines the context and intention of significant legislative changes–mainly additions and adjustments rather than simplifications–during the last fifty years. If such a preoccupation with historical events appears unnecessary, it should be recalled that forward-looking planners sometimes recall earlier planning *solutions* without always reassessing the *assumptions* specific to the earlier period. As Broadbent (1977) shows, policies devised in one economic phase may be implemented in contrasting conditions, and this is one contributory factor to the 'great planning disasters' chronicled by P. Hall (1980) in his book of that title.

The 1930s: still early days

Between the First and Second World Wars towns broke out of their most recent shell; the Victorian foot, omnibus, and railway suburbs, whether of villa or terrace, were to be left behind by the outward march of bicycle-, train-, and (in London) underground-commuters' semi-detached suburbs. Some, to be sure, would travel by car, but notice how few new houses were provided with garages. Planning was still haphazard, and supervised by the Ministry of Health. Not all of the 1,400 or more local authorities had yet encouraged developers to conform to simple land use zoning schemes. Councils frantically tried to build sufficient new schools in the burgeoning suburbs (especially around London; the other of the two nations, to the north, was experiencing chronic unemployment in traditional industries). Measures such as the Ribbon Development Act 1935 and the Green Belt Act 1938, both intended to prevent uncontrolled urban sprawl, especially around London, were applied too late.

The 1940s: the wartime view of peacetime

The military mind appreciates order and control. Operations, tactics, and strategy are key words in the language of military planning. War exposes civilian populations to regulations and restrictions, and shows them that economic and social 'targets' can be met by adherence to plans. Add this pervasive ethos to the natural desire to reconstruct blitzed cities to the best standards, and to build homes fit for heroes in a socially secure yet more egalitarian society, and the optimistic tone of wartime reports and plans can be appreciated.

To begin the decade, the delayed publication of the report (1940) of the Royal Commission on the Distribution of the Industrial Population, appointed in 1937 with Sir Anderson Mantague Barlow as chairman emphasized the grave social and strategical disadvantages of concentrating large numbers of people into a limited number of large conurbations. The commissioners advocated, in varying degrees, controls on the location of industry. After Barlow, the report of Lord Justice Scott's Committee on Land Utilization in Rural Areas (1942) urged the preservation of agricultural production in the countryside of the blockaded nation by a system of planning controls. The final report of the Expert Committee on Compensation and Betterment chaired by Lord Justice Uthwatt (1942) connected land use, planning controls, and land values, and urged the nationalization of undeveloped land.

Reports were followed by White Papers and then by legislation. Local authorities were empowered to reconstruct blitzed areas by the Town and Country Planning Act 1944. The Distribution of Industry Act 1945 empowered the Board of Trade to control the location of expanding factories through the Industrial Development Certificate (IDC). Following reports from Lord Reith's committee (1946), the New Towns Act of that year created new town development corporations which could operate at speed. Reports by John Dower (1945) and Sir Arthur Hobhouse's committee (1947) led to the National Parks and Access to the Countryside Act 1949 and creation of the National Parks Commission. The acquisition and management of national nature reserves was entrusted to the new Nature Conservancy.

But for our present purposes the most important provisions were those contained in the Town and Country Planning Act 1947, which established the mechanism for regulating the geography of change to *all* land and buildings. The system created by this Act is described in the next chapter; it is sufficient here to note that developers were now required to obtain planning permission for change from the local planning authority (normally a county or county borough council) which usually would be decided by reference to a statutory development plan. Development *land* had not been nationalized, as Uthwatt had urged; rather development *rights* over land had been nationalized. Safeguards against the arbitrary imposition of restrictions were afforded by the right of the public to object to the plan itself, and to appeal against the refusal of permission.

The 1950s: return of market forces

During the 1950s the planning-minded coalition and Labour governments of the previous decade were replaced by a Conservative government. The wartime shortages of food that led to rationing, and of construction materials that led to building licences, were soon to pass. Whereas the creators of the 1947 planning system had envisaged most development originating from public agencies, it was the private sector that was to prove dominant. Apart from the Town Expansion Act 1952, which allowed population overspill agreements to be made between large exporting cities and smaller receiving settlements, the decade brought few planning initiatives–and many would say regression. First, in 1953 the 1947 Act's 100 per cent development charge on land value increases arising through planning permission was abolished, and then after 1959 public authorities had to pay the *market* or *development value*, not the *existing use value*, of land acquired by compulsory purchase. (The difference between the two values may be considerable; a glance at a country newspaper might show agricultural land changing hands at £5,000 a hectare while the same land with outline planning permission for housing might be sold for £200,000 a hectare.) Goodall (1972) and Hallett (1979) explain the theory of land values, Ratcliffe (1976) recent policies, Massey and Catalano (1978) the structure of land ownership.

The 1960s: newcomers contemplating equity and growth

After the quiescent decade associated with Conservative government, there was another legislative effusion after a Labour government was returned in 1964. Several members of the new Cabinet sensed that they were makers of history, and turned their diaries, papers, and reminiscences into memoirs. George-Brown (1971) led the newly created and short-lived Department of Economic Affairs (1964–9), which produced both an unfortunately timed and misleadingly entitled *National Plan* in 1965 with forecasts by sectors, and also a more permanent regional structure for new economic councils and boards, modelled on prototypes in France and the USA. Richard Crossman (1975) gave his own view of the departmental and Cabinet battles while Minister of Housing and Local Government, 1964–6; his permanent secretary has also written about her department (Sharp, 1969).

The leitmotif of the decade was the search for managerial and technical methods of accommodating (and, in the search for equity, redistributing) the anticipated growth of population, and the related horrors of vehicle numbers, student numbers, office jobs in central London–at least until mid-decade–and demands on public water supplies. (See Inter-departmental Study Group, 1971; Buchanan, 1963; Robbins, 1963; Ministry of Housing and Local Government, 1964; and annual reports of the former Water Resources Board, respectively.) Growth brought increased pressures on the 'heritage', be it the coastline for which protection was proposed by the Countryside Commission (1968a and b, 1969), or attractive townscapes. 'Conservation areas' were given to the technical vocabulary by the Civil Amenities Act 1967 so that groups of buildings and their settings–not just isolated 'listed' buildings of architectural or historic interest–could be conserved. Old houses were offered reprieve from demolition by becoming rehabilitated new homes under the terms of the Housing Act 1969.

The development plan system seemed incapable of responding to such growth, and the Planning Advisory Group's report (1965) urged simplification and the identification of key issues. Machinery for the structure-plan/local-plan system was introduced in selected counties after the Town and Country Planning Act 1968. Bold desk studies showed how the anticipated growth pressures–for an extra twenty million or so Britons by the turn of the century–could be absorbed in, for example, South Hampshire, Deeside, Humberside, Severnside, the Scottish Central Borders, and Tayside. But while the prosperous southern estuaries flourished, economic planning councils in the North, North-West, and Yorkshire and Humberside, understandably felt almost overwhelmed by problems of obsolescence in housing, industry, public services, and transport networks. It was no comfort to be told that migration patterns were simply showing a reversion of migrants' interest to those parts of the country that were well favoured before the industrial revolution made kings of coal and cotton. Accordingly almost the whole of Britain outside the allegedly, but by no means uniformly, prosperous Midlands, South, and East was declared a 'development area' under the terms of the Industrial Development Act 1966, and economically sluggish areas, including much of Lancashire, south Yorkshire, and Humberside, were designated 'intermediate areas' after the Hunt Committee's recommendations (1969).

The 1970s: shocks, stagnation, and introspection

Reported at the time as a catastrophe, heralding a new era of political breakdown and economic diaster, the Yom Kippur war and OPEC oil price rises of 1973 certainly strained the world economic order. The shock waves of Bible-land hostilities were soon felt in England and Wales, which in 1974 were together undergoing a thorough reorganization of local government following the Local Government Act 1972. The pattern adopted almost totally disregarded the advice offered by the Redcliffe-Maud Royal Commission for England (1969). (New authorities were created in Northern Ireland in 1973 and in Scotland in 1975.) Ambitious, newly amalgamated councils had appointed well-paid officers in whose sparkling offices the new 'total approach' decision-makers had to contemplate at best stagnation and at worst unpopular public spending cuts (see the managerial proposals of the three 'making towns better' studies, Department of the Environment (DoE), 1973; for a view of the outcomes of corporate planning and community development see the critique by Cockburn, 1977). The structure planning system was now required of all counties, not just those selected experimentally after the 1968 Act. Alas, this proved no time for great expectations to be fulfilled.

Planners, accustomed to controlling the excesses of growth, now had to contemplate the realities of zero population growth and the casualties of recession–the unemployed, the vacated factory, or undeveloped site. Many shared a realization that much interventionist land use planning had not redistributed societal 'goods' to those in greatest need (Harvey, 1973).

The 'inner city' was rediscovered. Peter Shore, the fourth Secretary of State for the Environment (Peter Walker had energetically combined the ministries of Housing and Local Government, Transport, and Public Building and Works in 1970, see Draper, 1977), deflected the leviathan's research effort (additional inner area studies) and programme funding (rate support grant, urban aid, partnership schemes, grants under the Inner Urban Areas Act 1978) further in this direction. His department's urban affairs directorate also absorbed the earlier community development interests of the Home Office in a country which was belatedly recognizing the multi-racial composition of its major cities.

The organization of planning

In this summary of significant planning events, various agencies of government and some of the Acts of Parliament which define and legitimize their activities have been listed. Fig. 1 illustrates the organization of planning in England, omitting the eight counties and thirty-seven lower-tier districts in Wales, together with the nine regional councils, three all-purpose island authorities, and forty-nine district councils in Scotland, since the Secretary of State for Wales and the Secretary of State for Scotland function as the planning minister within their territories.

In England, then, the supervision and further development of land use planning rests with the DoE from which the Department of Transport (DTp) was partially released in 1976. Semi-permanent officials–for many civil servants are peripatetic–and even more briefly-posted politicians jointly devise legislation after the politicians have published their simplified election manifestos, and their generally more cautious White Papers when in office. The working of Acts is explained by circulars to local authorities, and design guides and policy notes can influence local practice even in the absence of new legislation. The departments of the

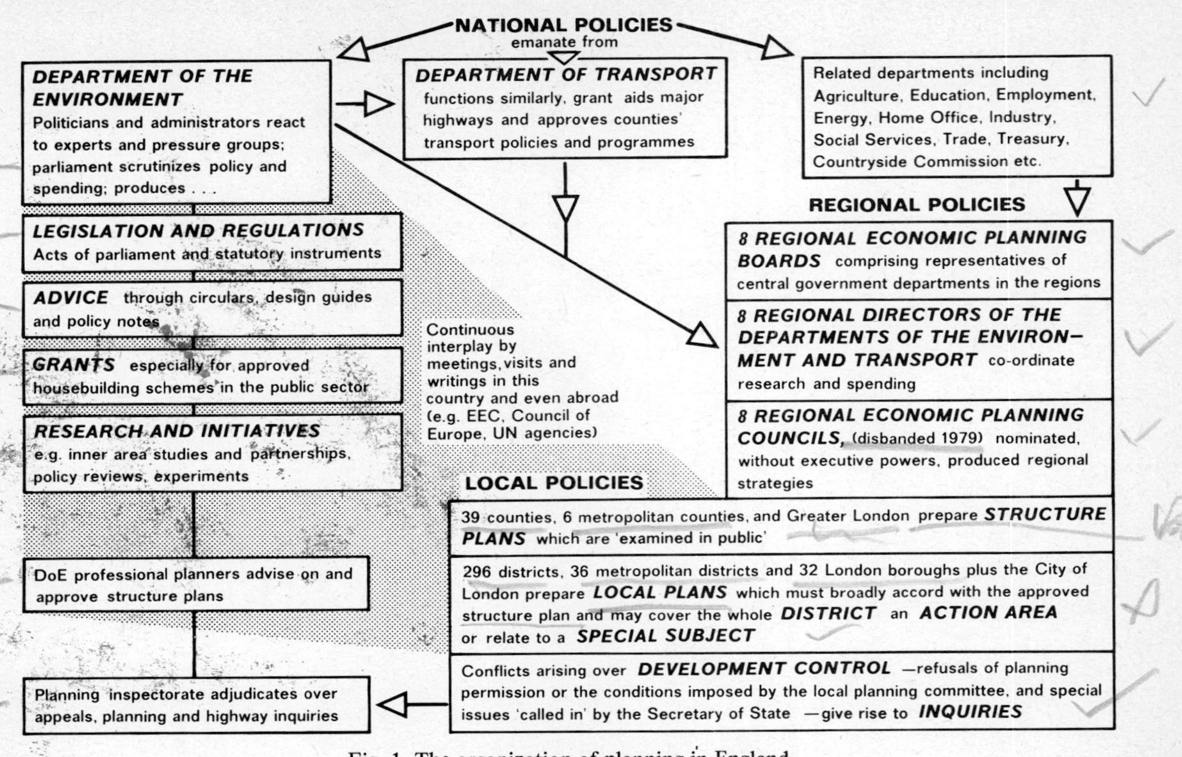

Fig. 1 The organization of planning in England.

Environment and of Transport conduct research, some internally, some through related agencies such as the Building Research Station and the Transport and Road Research Laboratory, and some by contracting with outside consultants, research institutes, universities, and polytechnics. Where departmental policies impinge on those of another department of state, accommodations may be reached by permanent secretaries acting for the minister, or by Cabinet committees. The department's day-to-day activities may be scrutinized by individual MPs asking questions; wider investigations of policy impacts and spending are made by select committees of MPs.

The two departments now share regional offices to co-ordinate infrastructure spending in the eight economic planning regions in England. Although there is no nationally agreed physical plan or diagram of the locations of future major investment, each of the regions produces a strategy document which does suggest the types and location of investment priorities. Although such strategies are more indicative than mandatory, they do influence the structure-plan makers in the English counties. The form, content, and means of approving plans is described more fully in the next chapter.

Further reading

Broadbent, T. A. (1977) *Planning and profit in the urban economy* (Methuen).

Central Office of Information (1979) *Environmental planning in Britain* (COI Reference Pamphlet 9, HMSO).

Cherry, G. (1974) *The evolution of British town planning* (Leonard Hill).

Cullingworth, J. B. (1976) *Town and country planning in Britain* (George Allen & Unwin).

Hall, P. (1975) *Urban and regional planning* (David & Charles; new edn. Penguin, 1980).

3 Plans and the geography of change

The post-1947 land use planning system in Britain, although largely forged during wartime when reconstruction was the dominant theme and when large population increases were not anticipated, has enjoyed almost three decades of addressing itself to accommodating growth and raised expectations. Physical growth in the numbers of people, houses and cars, and more space in the dwelling, the place of work, and for garaging and parking; growth of expectations in terms of disposable income and disposable leisure time. This chapter begins with a summary of the significant pressures for growth and the related zoning of parts of the country in the planners' attempt to direct or resist change. House (1977) describes the geography of change.

Pressures for growth

The planning system has partly constrained, yet partly acted in response to, the sum of individual people's movements in search of a change in housing or employment. In most planning studies the opening chapter plunders the Census of Population to examine locally those fundamental determinants of population change: births, deaths, and migration.

Natural change

The difference between births and deaths, 'natural change', was until 1977 positive in England and Wales as a whole. Indeed it has already started to rise again from this brief negative sojourn in the late 1970s (see Fig. 2). But even if total population numbers in many parts of the country show little change, there is a high continuing pressure on housing because of the increasing number of 'households'–people who share catering or a housekeeping budget. The numbers are difficult to find because statisticians variously report totals for England and Wales, or Great Britain, or the UK. But in Great Britain the number of one-person households rose from 1,563,000 in 1951 (10.7 per cent of all households) to 3,329,000 in 1971 (18.1 per cent of the much larger total).

The phenomenon of continuing housing pressure associated with the underoccupation of dwellings, often by the single elderly, and with overcrowding, especially in larger families with one earner, is common in many parts of Europe (Eversley, 1978). And most slum clearance schemes, replacing high density Victorian tenements and terraces with lower density public housing in which smaller families also occupy more rooms, have rarely led to a gain of housing units in inner cities. But there is a surprise. Although planning as conceived in the 1940s urged the decentralization of jobs and of population from congested

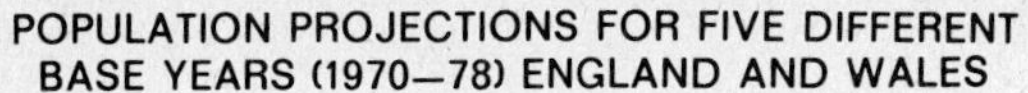

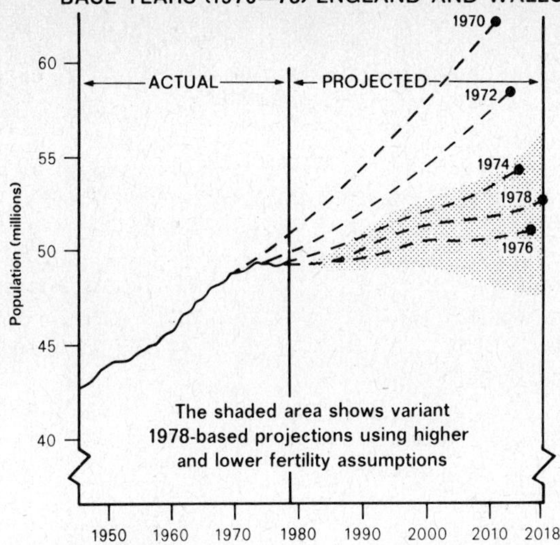

Fig. 2. Unfulfilled expectations of a rapidly increasing population in England and Wales. *Source: OPCS Monitor* PP2 77/1 and PP2 79/2 (*Crown copyright*)

conurbations, it has facilitated such movements with relatively small expansions to the area of developed land. Peter Hall and his co-workers have dubbed this the 'containment of urban England' (1973, summary and discussion 1974; also DoE, 1976). Often it has been achieved by rural counties reinforcing their political hostility to urban encroachment by the planning device of green belt designation. Two consequences follow as noted by Hall *et al.*–the separation of workplace and residence as new housing was developed in settlements beyond the edge of existing towns, and the scarcity of developable land which in part led to the unprecedented inflation of land and property values and often to a reduction in average dwelling and garden size compared with the 1930s.

It is easy, and has recently been fashionable, to blame 'the planners' directly for the decline of the inner city through the persistent out-migration of people and of firms. Certainly it is wrong to blame the new and expanding towns (NETs) programme for the total demise of industry in, say, inner London. The Department of Industry has estimated that about 135,000 manufacturing jobs were lost in London during the period 1966-74 (Economy Group, DSPSE Team, 1976). Removals to NETs accounted for about 11 per cent of these; 66 per cent were due to factory closures–more by deaths of firms than by 'marriages' or mergers. Interestingly, only 9 per cent of moves were to the assisted areas of the country; most stayed within or on the edges of the South East region.

Migration

So the current focus of interest in population change, given the small numerical gap between births and deaths in most parts of England and Wales, is migration. County-based population projections for the period 1977–91 for England alone (Campbell, 1979) suggest an absolute decrease for nine of England's forty-six counties (Greater London plus five of the six metropolitan counties: Greater Manchester, Merseyside, South Yorkshire, Tyne and Wear, West Midlands; together with Cumbria, East Sussex and Surrey). But NET policy has been important in particular counties in the past (Deakin and Ungerson, 1977) and may continue to be so. It accounted for the spectacular growth of 3.4 per cent p.a. in Hertfordshire in the period 1951–61, and 1.8 per cent p.a. in Hampshire, with its expanding town of Basingstoke, in the inter-census period 1961–71. Likewise, for 1977–91 predicted population growth rates averaging 12 per cent in the three counties of the East Anglia region arise principally from migration to officially-designated expanding towns in the region, and should not be greatly affected by the GLC's more recent attempted reversal of NET policy.

Because urban housing estates are better mapped and signposted, there is a tendency to overlook what is happening on industrial estates. More space is now given over to single storey factories, with their flow-line assembly lines and fork-lift trucks and even automated retrieval from storage racks. Space around them is provided for the access of long vehicles and for the parking of workers' cars. And as within homes, where space standards have been rising, so within the workplace. In offices especially, norms of space per clerical worker in the modern *Bürolandschaft* have been raised considerably. The pressures of large industrial projects on land, admittedly often on estuaries previously occupied exclusively by wildlife, have been documented by Willatts (1962), Beaver (1968) and Warren (1978).

Traffic demands

The atomization of households, and the concentration of fewer and larger manufacturing plants on city fringes, came during a period when car ownership became both desirable and attainable for the ordinary family. 'S'-shaped growth curves in the Buchanan report (1963) on *Traffic in towns* showed a projected increase in car ownership from 12 to 30 million vehicles between 1970 and 2010 (0.2 to 0.4 per head in a population rising from 54 to 74 million). The report suggested that saturation would occur by about 2010. Buchanan's team's basic thesis was that long before saturation, in the absence of restraint or environmental 'improvements', the car would destroy, and in some cases already had destroyed, the familiar fabric of town centres.

Larger regions became the focus for 'land use transportation (LU/T) studies'. In their infancy, and partly because initially the techniques were imported from car-dominated cities in the USA such as Chicago and Detriot, LU/T studies emphasized private road transport solutions. Drastic surgery by demolition is followed by a package of inner ring road, car park, and outer relief road construction as shown for twenty-eight British towns and cities by Amery and Cruickshank (1975), and also shown for remodelled city shopping centres by Davies (1977). Latterly the system of transport policies and programmes (TPPs), wherein counties annually submit to central government five-year rolling programmes for road building and maintenance and for investment in public transport, has meant that the complementarity of public and private transport is widely recognized.

Very often anticipated high growth did not materialize, or was postponed. For example, no levelling off in demand was evident from the Roskill Commission's (1971) projections of air passenger traffic through London's airports. Then the government abandoned the third London airport at Maplin (Department of Trade, 1974), the channel tunnel (HC *Debates*, 20 Jan. 1975, cols. 1023 and 1094–162), and announced cut-backs in support to local government services (DoE circular 171/74, 1974). For some observers, Britain and other western nations in the mid-1970s offered ample evidence that capitalism was moribund rather than just entering a post-industrial phase.

Pressures for preservation

Many 'conservationists' were relieved that economic stringencies at least reduced development pressures in the 1970s and helped to favour the rehabilitation of existing buildings. But the conservation movement is much more than simply a decade old (Sheail, 1976). Just as individuals often crave change at some times, stability at others, so with different parts of townscapes and landscapes. What one generation derides another may value–if it is given the chance.

In chapter 2 it was emphasized that the owner of property–land or buildings–in Britain can only undertake building works above a certain size, or materially change the use of land or premises, after obtaining planning permission. In old-style development plans which have been current since 1947, some areas of land appear shaded, others unshaded or 'white'. The shaded areas are those within which special policies will apply; the 'white areas' are those within which special safeguarding has not been designated and where agricultural uses are usually expected to dominate. The principal shaded areas are here described.

National parks number ten, and cover 1,362,000 ha (9 per cent) of England and Wales, mainly in the north and west, although the Hobhouse committee (1947) recommended two more in the Norfolk Broads and the South Downs, and Countryside Commission proposals for an eleventh in the Cambrian Mountains of mid-Wales were turned down by the Secretary of State for Wales. There are no national parks as such in

Scotland or in Northern Ireland. The ten are quite unlike the world's first national park (Yellowstone, USA, created in 1872) and those usually designated in other parts of the world, in that they are inhabited by villagers, foresters, hill farmers, and domesticated flocks. They are not strict nature reserves or inviolate wilderness areas. So developments do go ahead, often for controversial mineral working or power generation in addition to local housing schemes.

Generally speaking developments should not be at variance with the parks' two aims, the preservation and enhancement of natural beauty, and the provision of access and facilities for enjoyment by the public. Where these two aims clash, the former should dominate, said the national park policy review committee (Sandford, 1974). Several members of the Sandford committee urged the creation of national heritage areas–tracts of especially fine countryside in the parks within which land would be purchased by local or statutory authorities, or over which specific access agreements would be made, all with a view to preserving the familiar landscape. Other committee members dissented, fearing that the preferment of some areas would lead to the effective downgrading of others. Landscape elements are analysed in the national park plans–in effect structure plans–all of which were submitted during 1977–8.

Forest parks, designated by the Forestry Commission in several of their forests during the period 1936–57, offer facilities for public enjoyment, but cover only a small part of the commission's estate (J. Hall, 1974). *National nature reserves* in England and Wales are not extensive, few of the 150 or so exceed 5 km^2, but they function as a reminder that land can sometimes be managed primarily for the benefit and survival of indigenous flora and fauna. For an inventory of major biological sites see Natural Environment Research Council (1977).

Like national parks, *Areas of Outstanding Natural Beauty* (AONBs) are recommended for designation by the Countryside Commission, the body that by the Countryside Act 1968 superseded the National Parks Commission created by the National Parks and Access to the Countryside Act 1949. Whereas national parks usually comprise fairly remote and extensive uplands, AONBs in J. Dower's formulation (1945) are too small or 'humanized' to be considered for national park designation. There were thirty-three AONBs in England and Wales in 1978 (Countryside Commission, 1979) totalling 14,493 km^2 (9.6 per cent). The fact that much of the coastline of the south-west peninsula is AONB partly accounts for the region having nearly one-quarter of its area so classified. A further means of safeguarding coastlines is the 'heritage coast' appellation which derived from a series of regional conferences on coastal resources, pressures, and eyesores (National Parks Commission, 1967–8). By 1978 there were thirty-three stretches totalling 1,084 km. The final category of rural land shading, *Areas of High Landscape Value*, covers much of the Pennine uplands and the chalk lowlands of England.

Green belts have done much to contain urban England. They encircle Greater London and the six metropolitan counties, together with Bristol and Bath, Cambridge, Chester, Nottingham, Oxford, the Potteries of north Staffordshire, south Hampshire, and York. From modest calls for amenity parkland, green girdles, and tree-lined parkways, eventually came the Abercrombian metropolitan green belt, an annulus often extending 30 km or more from the edge of London's built-up area. As D. Thomas (1970) has shown, they are rarely green (containing as they do many 'urban' functions such as schools, playing fields, hospitals, sewage farms, electricity sub-stations), nor a true belt (because of the many pre-existing settlements that have often continued to grow within them). And although Alice Coleman (1977) accuses planners—including, of course, local politicians susceptible to local developers' suggestions—of not adhering strictly to the green belt principle by allowing scrappy 'rururban' infill, the belts have certainly kept building densities higher on the edge of towns. Without green belts and planning control, there is little doubt that British towns would have sprawled like inter-war Middlesex or like many American cities.

The point of all the above rural landscape classifications is not to prohibit any form of development within the designated area. Rather it is to ensure that approved development accords with strict standards of appearance and layout, and that would-be developers with inappropriate schemes in mind will be deterred even from making planning applications. In the late 1960s about 40 per cent of England and Wales fell into one or more of the five categories described, the extremes of regional variation being the East Midlands (13 per cent) and Northern region (69 per cent).

In addition to such broad zoning of often extensive tracts of countryside, means of protection can also be afforded to individual properties or to building groups. Buildings of 'special architectural or historic interest' are 'listed' by the DoE as a general means of safeguarding the appearance and of preventing demolition. Since the Civic Amenities Act 1967 local councils have also been able to designate 'conservation areas', groups of buildings in which the general character and settings are worthy of preservation. Notice of planning applications made in such areas is posted at or near the premises affected and printed in a local newspaper so that public comment may be weighed by the planning committee. Such preservation devices are more than aesthetic and nostalgic gestures; the conservation of buildings by refurbishment may be quicker and so less expensive than demolition and rebuilding, even for City of London offices (Lloyd, 1976).

Resuscitating the inner city

In residential areas the rehabilitation of older property was given parliamentary approval by the Housing Act 1969. Its preceding White

Paper (Cmnd. 3602), 'Old houses into new homes', recognized the short-term economic pressures for extending a property's life span, but it came at a time when there was widespread denunciation in the press of the miseries of badly constructed and maintained high-rise family dwellings, of the social dislocation and physical annihilation of diversity of function associated with clearance schemes. So rehabilitation implied social and physical continuity in traditional street layouts with their demarcated and, as we now know to call them, defensible spaces. Newman (1976) observed that vandalism was lower on those New York public estates where design had reduced the confusion of residents and passers-by about who was allowed on which spaces around dwellings. Landlords, owner-occupiers, and public authorities were encouraged to rehabilitate. Housing improvement grants were offered by local authorities, although as no student of the delivery of state services and cash benefits will be surprised to find, the properties occupied by families in the greatest need were rarely those benefiting from grants (Duncan, 1974; see also Tenth Report from the Expenditure Committee HC 349, 1972-3). After the 1969 Act local authorities delineated General Improvement Areas (GIAs) within which the importance of the environment outside the home–trees, paving, parking spaces, playspace, traffic management–was recognized as being no less a contribution to the congeniality of an area than the internal structure, condition, and amenity provision of housing (the *Deeplish study*, Ministry of Housing and Local Government (MHLG) 1966, is the forerunner of such 'area improvements'). Further categories of Housing Action Areas (HAAs) and adjacent Priority Neighbourhoods were introduced in 1974 with the purpose of directing public funds to areas of housing stress, usually compounded of shared facilities in overcrowded accommodation rented by poor families. The means of delimiting such areas by population census indicators is described in the DoE's *Area Improvement Note* 10 (1975).

At a larger geographical scale than HAAs and GIAs, large tracts of the older urban areas of England and Wales have been designated as 'partnership' or 'programme' areas under the Inner Urban Areas Act 1978. This Act followed the inner cities White Paper (Cmnd. 6845, 1977) in which Peter Shore as the then Environment Secretary heralded new government initiative and spending in favour of the inner city, partly by slowing the growth of new and expanding towns. He also captured the role of inner city 'lead agency' for the DoE, which had earlier been overshadowed by the Home Office's community development programme. The hurriedly prepared inner cities White Paper and related ministerial speeches relied heavily on the emerging findings of the three inner area study teams working in Liverpool's Granby and Edge Hill district, Birmingham's Small Heath, and London's Stockwell. Problems of housing decay and unemployment were common to all three areas, and the consultants' reports (DoE, 1977) variously urged the channelling of resources to areas and people in greatest need, means of resuscitating the areas' dwindling economic bases, a mixture of small-scale rehabilitation and redevelopment, improved service organization and delivery, and generally more sensitive urban government, and (in London especially) help for would-be migrants to leave the inner city for the outer suburbs or elsewhere. Such tasks were largely accepted by the new 'partnership' committees of central and local government.

So in the decades since the physical planner introduced Comprehensive Development Areas (CDAs), the planners of education and welfare services have likewise espoused an 'area-based' approach to the concentration of resources in *areas* of greatest need. From the Plowden Report (1967) came 'education priority areas'; the Home Office declared immigrant priority areas. GIAs and HAAs date from the same period. Critics then started asking if the drawing of boundaries for priority areas was catching most of the *people* in greatest need. Townsend (1976) certainly thought not, and was supported by Berthoud's (1976) analysis of rarely-obtainable income data derived from the unexpected source of household interviews for an updated land use–transportation study in London. So the current orthodoxy is that area-based policies often fail to help those people in greatest need, and that negative income tax for those beneath the elusive (but all-too-present) poverty line, or a minimum statutory wage, would bring greater relief to both the urban and the less conspicuous rural poor (see Hamnett, 1979).

Grades of regions

Similar criticisms have been levelled at British regional policy. After the 1979 general election Conservative MPs criticized the blanket designation of development areas introduced by the then Labour government in 1966 and which by mid-1979 covered about 45 per cent of the working population of Great Britain. Only in south-east and midland England were industrial investors unaided. The Conservatives favoured reducing the population covered by assisted area status (special development area, development area, and intermediate area) to about 25 per cent over three years or so, thereby making central government aid for new plant and machinery, and buildings and works, more selective (Department of Industry 1980 tabulates the changes; see HC *Debates*, 17 July 1979, cols. 1302–21 and *Written Answer*, cols. 480–96).

The special development areas have changed little from those coal-mining, shipbuilding, and steel-making areas identified in the 1930s as requiring special government assistance to combat chronic unemployment. Even—or should one say especially?—nationalization (i.e. centralization of accounting?) has done little to stem factory closures. The declaration of most of Scotland, Wales, northern and south-western England as development areas in 1966 marked a significant departure from the previous pattern of aiding restricted localities where unemployment rates exceeded about 4.5 per cent of the working population. Intermediate areas, championed in Sir Joseph Hunt's committee report of 1969 (Cmnd. 3998), were those parts of the country with sluggish industries such as pottery, glass, textiles, which also needed a face-lift and image enhancement. Successive governments have tried to steer 'footloose' manufacturing industry to the development areas through grants and loans, and have only latterly recognized the importance of service industries to regional economic structure. On reviewing regional development incentives in 1973 the House of Commons Expenditure Committee (HC 85, 1973–4) was sceptical of the benefits of (then) pumping about £400m. a year into a few mobile firms when some 95 per cent of firms' expansion take place adjacent to the existing premises.

The control of change by plans

So far, some of the pressures for population growth, for visual preservation, and for urban and industrial resuscitation at various scales have been summarized. The means whereby policies are described and applied to places where the pressures are felt is 'the plan', usually a map or more abstract cartogram and related text, which zones an administrative unit into policy areas. Planning's protagonists and parliamentary drafters in the 1940s envisaged a straightforward system in which the central Ministry of Town and Country Planning would 'secure consistency and continuity in . . . a national policy [for] the use and development of land throughout England and Wales', partly by approving the local planning authorities' development plans. Such plans were introduced by the Town and Country Planning Act 1947 as a means of 'indicating the manner in which a local planning authority propose that land in their area should be used'. County maps were at the scale of 1:63,360 (one-inch), and county borough and other town maps at 1:10,560 (six-inch) scale with occasional insets of comprehensive development areas (CDAs) at 1:2500 (25-inch) scale.

Development plans emerged after a full survey and analysis of an authority's geographical endowment and development potential. Some of the best of the 'reports of survey', although stylized and categorized, show a lively appreciation of the geographer's traditional methods of regional description and analysis. Draft plans were available for at least six weeks' public inspection; objections might be heard at a public inquiry, and the ministry's modifications would be submitted locally before final approval and publication. Development plans viewed a twenty-year time horizon and were supposed to be updated quinquennially. For example, the old London County Council's development plan was published in draft in 1951, provoked 6,700 objections, many of which were aired at the 1952 public inquiry, and after approval was published for public purchase in 1955. The first quinquennial review in 1960 was likewise approved in 1962, and as most post-1965

London boroughs were still preparing local plans at the end of the 1970s it has had to serve London too long as a detailed development plan.

Mindful also of the static nature of development plans, not just their prolonged birth and longevity, the Planning Advisory Group's report (1965) on the future of development plans urged a new two-tier system of plan-making which was adopted by the Planning Act of 1968. The higher-tier authority (counties and some national parks in England and Wales since the 1974 reorganization) would prepare a *structure plan* (see MHLG 1970). Although it pays regard to broad economic and social conditions, its primary purpose is to establish policy and general proposals for development and land use in the plan area, including the improvement of the physical environment and traffic management. It looks outwards to the approved regional strategies, and also provides the framework for detailed local plans. At the outset the public–individuals and organizations–are invited to respond to the findings about key issues and alternative solutions that are contained in the 'report of survey'. Following the public's expressed views, and consultations with government departments and adjoining authorities, the list of contents is established and further publicized. Once the structure plan is prepared it is submitted to the planning minister who will usually arrange for an 'examination in public' of the major unresolved issues. This examination, usually of three to six weeks' duration, allows discussion in front of an impartial panel rather than the antagonistic interrogation of 'objectors' in the old development plan system. After the minister's proposed modifications have been publicized and debated, the structure plan is finally agreed (see figure 4 in chapter 4).

Unlike the structure plan's 'key diagram' and 'written statement', the lower tier's *local plan* (compiled by districts since 1974) does include a proposals map on an Ordnance Survey base which shows the effect of the structure-planning intentions for individual land holdings. Local plans share the structure-plan sequence of publicity, public participation, and official consultation. They may be of three forms. *District plans*, like the old development plans, show the totality of planning factors as they affect the district area. Like the comprehensive development area plans that they replace, *action area plans* relate to smaller areas, such as shopping centres, which the council has selected for intensive change, whether by development, renewal, improvement or a combination of all three. *Subject plans* treat particular themes such as conservation, or tourism, or mineral extraction, or a small village, and to compound public confusion any particular part of a local authority district might feature in more than one local plan. Unlike structure plans, local plans are subject to a formal public inquiry in front of an inspector, but they do not now require the approval of the planning minister.

The final suite of plans, the *regional strategies* for each of the eight former economic planning regions in England, has had the highest level of indeterminacy. As many major public and private investment decisions show a 'lead time' of up to ten years before the first tentative idea is turned finally into a visible structure, regional plans have surveyed possible trends ten to twenty years in the future. Most of the planning regions followed the sequence from an early fact-finding planning study to the formulation of a regional strategy in the 1970s by a tripartite team jointly composed of local and central government planners and staff of the region's economic planning council, partly as a means of forestalling suspicion in the region of Whitehall's intentions. But especially because of the inter-departmental structure of economic planning boards and the wide representation of interests on appointed economic planning councils (see Fig. 1) the regional strategy has been a useful summary of the location of investment intentions by central government departments. It has also highlighted variations in regional public expenditure, and hinted at the additional environmental and social costs and benefits of alternative development patterns. But the tenses in this paragraph, alas, should be past perfect not present perfect: the regional economic planning councils were disbanded in 1979, although the economic planning boards survive.

How, then do these various plans affect the geography of change? Several preliminary points need emphasis. First, plans have reached a different state of completion, or have ceased to be fresh at differing rates, in different parts of the country. For example, at the end of 1978 examinations in public had been started or completed for seventeen out of the twenty-three structure plans expected to emerge in the West Midlands region; the South-West had none out of eleven (Morrison, 1978). Plans being compiled then could incorporate the gloomy prospect of energy shortages, and so resurface ideas on combined heat and power from power stations; those that went before were largely unaware of the energy-using implications of alternative urban layouts and transport options. (Remember that some counties were allowed to establish structure-plan teams after the 1968 Planning Act; others were assembled in earnest after the 1974 administrative reorganization.) The timeliness of believed political advantage accounts in part for the propensity of planning committees to adhere to portions of the plan when it suits them, and almost to forget it when it does not. In periods of high unemployment, job-generating developments are eagerly sought by every local authority.

Second, structure-planning teams also vary in their sophistication and technical expertise. Some include planners versed in modern analytical and computational methods for connecting changes in population, housing, employment, and transport. Others might find systems-thinking rather daunting. Aggressive planning departments might have used the structure plan experience as the means of furthering an authority's corporate plan-making, just as some planners see their training as allowing them to understand how to plan anything, not simply land use and settlements. So plans can say as much about their professional compilers and political editors as about the area that they investigate.

Third, the official vision of a brighter future is rarely radical. Even though the preliminary work of, for example, the North-West and Northern strategy teams was severely critical of then prevailing modes and levels of government financial support to their regions, planners and their political partners broadly accept that the land market will function much as it has, that the burden of taxation will change little, that family structures are unlikely to be exploded, and so forth. Mile-high cities and methane-producing communes do not leap out of approved written statements.

At present, plans exist for the regions but their status is rather uncertain; some 40 per cent of structure plans had been approved by 1978, but few local plans have reached public inquiry stage. Yet it is at a local scale that planning bites. Most of us are only stirred into opposing changes if they affect our immediate surroundings. Local plans show the several categories of protected land listed earlier in this chapter. They also show what will be generally allowed as the future land uses in an authority's area. Usually a new plan proposes a minor resorting of land uses to remove non-conforming uses from residential areas and to enlarge open-space corridors or complexes, and allocates farmland for housing development. So the plan shows a potential builder, converter, or developer of any kind where to look for investment opportunities, and where to expect to be refused.

Figure 3 shows the sequence of development control whereby an application for planning permission for 'building, engineering or other operations', or for 'changes of use' is processed. Naturally a serious applicant for planning permission will, either directly or through his retained professional architect or surveyor, normally discuss informally the form and location of his proposed development before submitting a formal planning application. So the number of actual planning applications in Table 2 severely underestimates the number of schemes first thought of by developers. But a tenacious and wily developer will sometimes secure planning permission in the most unexpected places. The student of planning decisions therefore soon learns to view the old development plan or new local plan as an advisory document—a view of an intended future state seen from some starting-point, and not a mandatory and immutable future state.

During most of the 1960s and 70s the number of planning applications in England and Wales fell in the range 400,000–470,000 p.a., with exceptional peaks in 1972 (615,000) and 1973 (623,000). Refusal rates averaged about 17 per cent, but would commonly exceed 20 per cent in national parks, and were nearer 30 per cent in green belts. But as the House of Commons Expenditure Committee's rather exasperated second report on planning procedures pointed out in 1978 (HC 564,

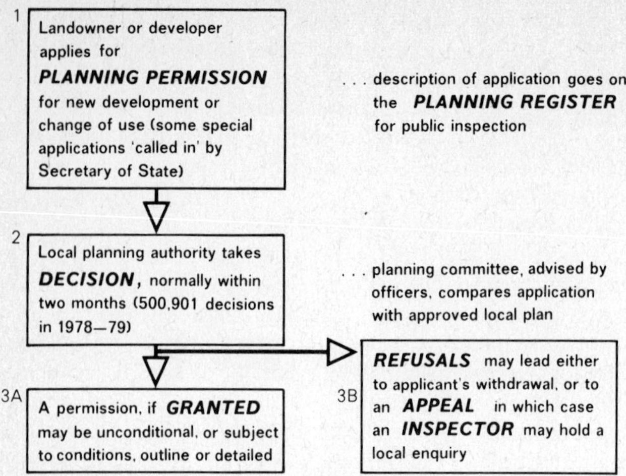

Fig. 3 The sequence of development control under the Town and Country Planning Acts. (Road proposals are decided under the Highways Acts 1959 and 1971; see Cmnd. 7132 and 7133, 1978.)

TABLE 2 *Planning applications in England and Wales, 1978/79*: number of decisions by class of development†*

Class of development	No. of decisions	Permissions granted No.	Permissions granted %	Appeals No.	Appeals % allowed
A Building, engineering and other operations	450,318	393,073	87	6,968	26
of which					
1 Residential	107,768	80,037	74	3,995	19
2 Industrial, storage, and warehousing	25,509	22,693	89	318	40
3 Offices	8,918	7,838	88	124	41
4 Retail distribution and servicing	21,422	18,374	86	245	31
5 Mineral working	631	509	81	26	39
6 All other classes of building and other operations	286,070	263,622	92	2,260	34
B Changes of use	50,583	39,497	78	2,602	33
Total: all classes of development (**A+B**)	500,901	432,570	86	9,570	28

* Financial year ends 31 March.

† Includes provisional figures for the County of Clwyd.

Source: Department of the Environment/Welsh Office (1980) *Development control statistics*, tables 2, 3, 30, 31.

1977–8), little is known about the extent to which shadings of landscape protection actually lead to higher quality development. Table 2 gives the number of decisions and appeals for 1978/9 within the two main categories of new development and changes of use. Applications reflect wider economic fortunes: the number of applications for petrol stations declined from 8,470 in 1965 to 3,367 in 1975/6.

Planning displeases Parliament

Reasons for, and the cost to the public of, delays in processing planning applications and determining appeals were the subject of Parliament's first report on planning procedures (Eighth Report from the Expenditure Committee, session 1976–7, HC 395–I). In 1976 nearly two-fifths of the 17,500 local authority planning staff were engaged in development control, and consumed a similar proportion of the £104m. budget for administering planning. A comprehensive review of planning was requested in the report. The Labour government refused (Cmnd. 7056, 1978), saying that the structure planning system was only partially operational. In reply the committee's eleventh report (HC 564, 1977–8) disagreed. When would structure plans be completed? How were the two tiers of planning related? Exactly what did regional planning do? Why indeed compile development plans if half of the 'green field' housing development has taken place on land not formally zoned for it (HC 564, Q. 39, p. 21)?

As in so many fields of public administration–and private business–the practitioners appear, understandably, to be too busy to review the effect of their actions. By claiming work overloadings, local authorities fended off the DoE's proposed annual recording of land use changes and planning approvals in relation to a new national land use classification (DoE, 1975). A general information system for planning, GISP, is more in evidence in manuals than in operation, although some counties have adopted sophisticated land use data banks as shown in an Experimental Cartography Unit survey (NERC, 1978). Certainly the post-1979 Conservative government has little interest in promoting national surveys for their own sake. For example, it supports surveys of vacant public land in particular localities in order to speed its redevelopment.

In the absence of an improved recording system the raw totals of Table 2 tell us naught of how planning approvals will change our surroundings, add, relocate, or remove jobs, increase or reduce the dwelling stock. The table more fairly records a bureaucratic work load. It includes errors of classification, double counting of outline and detailed consents, and the allocation of complex urban multiple-use developments into the dominant category. And not all planning approvals materialize in development. Outline permissions automatically expire after three years, detailed ones after five years, but renewal can be sought by a new application. A national sample survey of land which in July 1975 had outstanding planning permission for private residential development showed that work had started on about 70 per cent of sites by 1977; there was no activity on 25 per cent, and the remaining 5 per cent had been misclassified (DoE, 1978).

Further reading

Statistical sources

J. T. Coppock and L. F. Gebbett (1978) *Land use and town and country planning* (Pergamon, for Royal Statistical Society and Social Science Research Council).

Central Statistical Office, *Regional Statistics* (HMSO, annually).

Department of the Environment, *Development Control Statistics* (DoE Statistics Planning and Regional Division, annually).

Office of Population Censuses and Surveys, *Population Trends* (HMSO, quarterly).

County and district plans and related decisions

Examination of the old-style development plans, and new structure and district plans, for any familiar county in England and Wales will show the changing intent and methods of planning authorities. Details of individual planning applications and decisions on them are placed in a 'planning register', public access to which is safeguarded by law (see the Town and Country Planning Association's *Planning Aid Leaflets*: No. 2, 'Using the planning register'; No. 3, 'How to make representations on an application for planning permission'; No. 4, 'Your right to attend planning committee meetings' (all 1978)). Samples of planning application and appeal forms are reproduced in J. Ardill (1974) *The new citizen's guide to town and country planning* (Charles Knight, for Town and Country Planning Association).

Regional plans

Likewise the sequence of regional study to strategy should be examined for a familiar region. In the South East, for example, the sequence is as follows:

Ministry of Housing and Local Government (1964) *The South East study: 1961–1981* (HMSO).

South East Economic Planning Council (1967) *A strategy for the South East* HMSO).

South East Joint Planning Team (1970) *Strategic plan for the South East* (HMSO).

South East Joint Planning Team (1976) *Strategy for the South East: 1976 review* (HMSO).

Department of the Environment (1978) *Strategic plan for the South East review: government statement* (HMSO).

For a planning councillor's interpretation of their meanings see P. Hall (1980) 'The life and death of a quasi quango: the South East Planning Council', *London Journal* 6, 196–206.

4 Planning people's places

As recently as thirty years ago 'planning' was synonymous with creations and actions that were almost universally regarded as desirable: slum clearance allied with comprehensive redevelopment on neighbourhood lines and the plantation of new towns beyond city fringes contained by green belts; the designation of national parks; through development control the eradication of the anarchy of a scatter of pepper-pot bungalows in the countryside, ribbon development and unsightly hoardings. Nowadays planning and planners are popularly associated with the undesirable: estates of high-rise blocks in the bulldozed inner city or, at the city's fringe, bulldozed farms at the end of infrequently-served bus routes; blighting and intruding urban motorways; multi-storey car parks in the stead of multi-purpose local shops and small industrial premises . . . Planning has come to imply an alien and insensitive order imposed on a jumbled urban fabric and a confused electorate suspicious of change.

More than ever, planners and politicians have now to acknowledge that the public–or citizens in the American parlance–will often expect to be involved in proposals that affect their familiar neighbourhoods or cherished landmarks and landscapes, and certainly demand to be involved in anything that affects their 'peace, quiet and property values' –in a phrase typical of H. J. Gans. Pressures for involvement were well summarized by Meyerson and Banfield (1955) in their study of Chicago public housing scheme locations: 'Decisions regarding locations, along with decisions regarding budget amounts, are the form in which city planning usually comes into political focus (a comprehensive plan as such is almost never the subject of serious political discussion or action)'.

In Britain protest may start with the individual householder aggrieved at the refusal of planning permission (see the hypothetical case studies assembled by the Local Government Training Board, 1977), or by a neighbour who has been notified officially about the building intentions, and told by the same local planning authority where to inspect the plans and how to object if necessary. Increase the numbers of aggrieved citizens to the neighbourhood and we find spontaneously-formed or longer-established groups protesting variously about demolition for comprehensive urban renewal or commercial redevelopment, or middle-class 'gentrifiers' acquiring formerly working-class housing, or a neighbourhood's meriting of the appellation 'General Improvement Area', or roads, lead factories, a bus lane outside a shopping parade, or whatever. The canny aggrieved will have bought a primer on protesting (e.g. C. Hall, 1974) or even raised £57,000 mainly to hire skilled counsel to spare Cublington from razing by a third London airport (Perman, 1973). Chroniclers, as frequently participant observers or environmental correspondents as academic voyeurs, have charted battles of the David (initially inarticulate locals) versus Goliath (the property developers in cahoots with the council-as-developer) variety: e.g. Christensen (1979) and Anson (1981) for Covent Garden; Wates (1976) for Tolmers Square; Gladstone (1976) for selected provincial cities; Amery and Cruickshank (1975) for many town centres; Aldous (1972) for town and countryside.

National pressure groups

Theses have been written on typologies of pressure groups–their recruitment, organization and effectiveness–but little work has been done on their location. The charge is usually made that groups are to be found where the articulate and group-forming middle classes are found, and certainly the perceived vigour of local civic societies registered with the Civic Trust (200 in 1957, 1,280 in 1976; see Civic Trust, 1976) appears greater in towns with a good proportion of professional residents or of 'delocalized residents' (to use H. G. Wells's neologism for commuters). The late Tony Crosland (1971) characterized the conservationist lobby members as being 'often kindly and dedicated people . . . [they are] affluent and fundamentally, though of course not consciously, they want to kick the ladder down behind them.'

The Civic Trust was founded in 1957 to 'encourage high quality in architecture and planning; eliminate and prevent ugliness . . . and stimulate public interest'. It has organized demonstration schemes such as the pedestrianization of London Street, Norwich, the cheering up of façades in Burslem, Staffordshire, and regional action against eyesores and decay in the North East. It was the driving force behind the Civic Amenities Act 1967 which allowed for the designation of 'conservation areas' in which setting and surroundings are preserved, not just individual buildings. Similarly, the Friends of the Earth (FOE) and Conservation Society function with a central policy and information unit supporting local branches. In contrast, support for the Town and Country Planning Association derives from individual subscribing members scattered over the country. Formed in 1899 as the Garden Cities Association to promote Ebenezer Howard's vision of the mystical union of the best from town and country, the TCPA still lobbies for the new towns, but also for reduced settlement densities, and for wider planning reforms as discussed in its monthly journal *Town and Country Planning*.

Protest in more strident forms is often encountered: it proliferates now in posters, on placards, and at boisterous public meetings in crumbling neighbourhoods. *Community Action* newspaper records the grievances and tactics of countless local groups. To be sure, some protests are fertile fields for 'advocacy planners', often young professional or student planners contacted through citizens' advice bureaux, neighbourhood law centres, planning aid schemes such as the TCPA's, or too rarely via the shop-front premises occupied by some enterprising local planning authorities. The advocates may challenge a council's delivered orthodoxy, promote alternative schemes, and engender community identity. Members of the architects' and surveyors' professional institutions have likewise sensed that they certainly recruit from, and very often serve, quite a narrow spectrum of social classes.

Political scientists are interested in broader questions about when and how the public are involved in policy-making and implementation. The past decade has seen many initiatives–and not a few failures–in worker participation in industrial management, more representative school governing bodies, student representation on college governing bodies, and so forth. But land use planning as enshrined in the 1947 Act has for over three decades safeguarded the citizen's right to *object* to a draft development plan before it is approved by the planning minister. Generally, of course, most objections are generated by the most controversial and usually most disruptive ingredients of plans–large-scale demolitions and new roads. Thereafter it still remains for an adjudicating minister or local politician to ponder the observation of Samuel Taylor Coleridge that men have to be weighed, not counted. Weighing conflicting evidence through public inquiries is analysed by Wraith and Lamb (1971).

In many ways the receiving of objections reinforces the negativism inherent in development *control*–which implies the prohibition of bad development rather than the promotion of the good. A code of practice for the examination in public of structure plans (DoE/Welsh Office, 1973) introduced this novel 'probing discussion, covering not only arguments critical of the plan but also representations supporting it, instead of the formalized procedures of the traditional inquiry into objections'. An independent chairman, supported by an examination panel, replaces the public inquiry inspector.

A sensitive and sensible planning authority will not, of course, produce plans that run entirely counter to local feelings. Not only will it have elicited public views–the so-called 'induced participation' of applause or opprobrium, or in George Dobry's view (1975) 'public consultation'–but it should have encouraged 'indicative participation' which is Dobry's understanding of public participation as the public's active involvement from the outset in the formulation of plans and the making of major decisions. An idealized view of the planning process (Fig. 4) incorporates direct public involvement at all but the most technical stages of plan preparation, and even here remember that elected politicians will be scrutinizing the professional planners' actions.

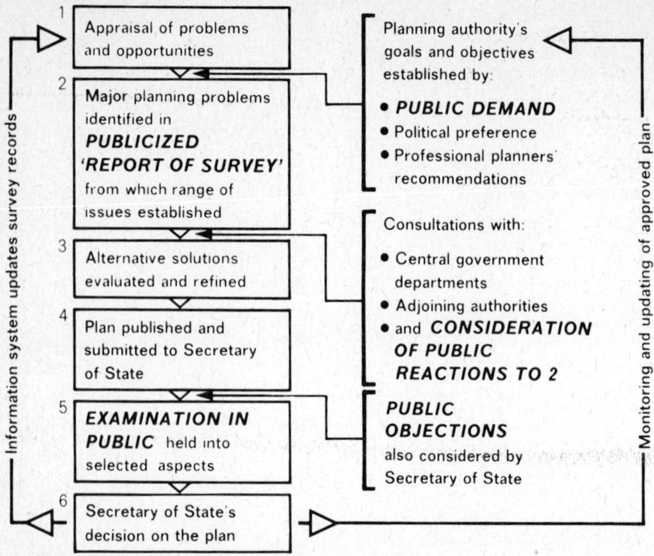

Fig. 4 Public involvement in structure planning in England and Wales, with the more active stages of public involvement shown in bold type. *After* S. McConnell, *Official Architecture and Planning* 32 (1969), p. 1501.

Participation after Skeffington

The official British primer on the subject, the Report of the Committee on Public Participation in Planning is rarely known by its cover title, *People and planning*, but by its chairman, Arthur M. Skeffington, MP (1969). Skeffington's committee considered 'the best methods, including publicity, of securing the participation of the public at the formative stage in the making of development plans for their area'. It concluded that structure-plan preparation should be accompanied by meetings, exhibitions, and wide publicity. Likewise authorities preparing local plans should publicize their proposed programme and present the relevant structure-plan decisions to the public.

Two enabling mechanisms were suggested. First, community forums might be established to 'provide local organizations with the opportunity to discuss collectively planning and other issues of importance to the area'. Second, community development officers should be appointed 'to secure the involvement of those people who do not join organizations'. There are also those who are rarely heard–children (see Ward, 1979), cyclists, and pedestrians (Hillman and Whalley, 1972) especially. Neither forums nor officers for community development have come to pass in the numbers or form intended and this in spite of the Liberal Party's support of community politics and wider interest in neighbourhood councils for small areas in the urban mass, in the late 1960s.

Worse perhaps is the commonly expressed view that few local governments have shown particular expertise in successfully involving the public, which leads naturally to Damer and Hague's conclusion (1971) that participation in planning alone is meaningless without more participation in political life and a consequent redistribution of power.

A growth in participatory democracy at the expense of representative democracy has been noticed in many countries. Citizens' protests against nuclear power stations in West Germany are cited as examples of *Bürgerinitiative.* Such protests are made because many feel that elected politicians neither share their views, nor even can be relied on faithfully to transmit them to policy-making and executive agencies. Politicians may, of course, be publicizing their differences from the opposing party, or, as individuals, seeking position in the party as much as electors' votes, which is partly why Hampton's survey (1970) of the importance of local issues in Sheffield showed such differences between electors and elected. Both groups rated housing issues highly; but whereas over one-half of electors mentioned roads and traffic as important local issues, less than one-fifth of councillors so responded. We might note in passing that participation might perplex many councillors. Are pressure groups more or less representative than the ballot box? Who will speak for the mute and unsupported neighbourhoods? Need and ability to shout may not coincide.

Local government made more remote

The waxing of participatory democracy has coincided with the reform of local government in the UK, outside Greater London, in the period 1973-5. W. A. Robson (quoted in Mackintosh, 1968) had noted that in the 1950s many authorities were too small to provide adequate services, disputes about overspill schemes were common between counties and inlier county boroughs, and many services for large areas were entrusted to *ad hoc* appointed, not popularly elected, bodies.

It took the Royal Commission on Local Government in England (chairman Rt. Hon. Lord Redcliffe-Maud) the three years 1966-9 to recommend possible authorities, boundaries, and functions in areas of varying character that would best satisfy the compromise between economic efficiency (larger preferred) and effective local democracy (smaller preferred). After painstaking research, the majority report (Cmnd. 4040) recommended fifty-eight all-purpose 'unitary areas' and three metropolitan areas. In his compendious memorandum of dissent (Cmnd. 4040-I), Derek Senior advocated five provincial councils above thirty-five regional authorities, subdivided into 148 district authorities. At the lowliest level, common councils would be those 'existing parishes, towns, and parts of towns small enough to have a real feeling of community'. Interestingly for planners concerned with neighbourhood identity, definitions of 'home area' revealed by the commission's community-attitudes survey (Cmnd. 4040-II, appendix 7) seemed to be the whole settlement for towns of 30,000 or less, but only a group of streets according to respondents in cities of 250,000 or more inhabitants. Cognate sociological literature on community identification is reviewed by Bell and Newby (1978).

The commissioning Labour government broadly accepted Maud's proposals in 1970 (Cmnd. 4276, 1970), the incoming Conservatives did not (Cmnd. 4584, 1971). Although at 332 the number of English lower-tier districts created by the Local Government Act 1972 was one-third of those swept away, the counties remained largely intact, preserving, in H. G. Wells's phrase of 1903, 'the essential conceptions of a vanished organization'. Maud's and Senior's demarcation of varying sizes of city regions–or 'daily urban systems' in an American phrase–as sensible units within which to plan services was not followed. Formerly proud county boroughs such as Bristol, Hull, and Nottingham, reduced to the status of county districts, outside the new metropolitan counties, felt themselves stripped of rightful powers. The Labour government in 1979 announced that some powers might be returned to them (Cmnd. 7457), but a complete overhaul of the new system cannot be expected for some decades. The regional tier of government was carefully considered by the later Royal Commission on the Constitution 1969–73 (eventual chairman Lord Kilbrandon), but after referendum voters showed little enthusiasm for elected assemblies in Scotland and in Wales, the aspirations of English regions for their own tier of elected government–with strategy formulation and budgets?–were cut short.

So electors now find themselves represented by fewer councillors meeting in more remote council chambers. An opportunity to increase the fairness of local government spending patterns, both between areas and among individuals, by means of a local income tax discussed in the 1976 report of the Committee of Inquiry on Local Government Finance (chairman Frank Layfield, QC) has not been taken. Such a locally raised tax would have forced people to come to terms with the new local government pattern more than do exhortations to 'give us your views on this structure plan'. Meyerson and Banfield were correct: budget debates do excite public interest.

Further reading

A. Barker, comp. (1979) *Public participation in Britain: a classified bibliography* (Bedford Square Press/Royal Town Planning Institute).

J. F. Garner *et al.* (1979) 'Policy forum: Skeffington revisited', *Town Planning Review* 50, 412–36.

P. Hain, ed. (1976) *Community politics* (Calder).

R. Kimber and J. Richardson, eds. (1974) *Campaigning for the environment* (Routledge).

W. R. D. Sewell and J. T. Coppock, eds. (1977) *Public participation in planning* (Wiley).

5 Case studies of planned major changes

This chapter adopts a case study approach. Some of the six case studies have aroused considerable public attention–usually in the form of a prolonged statutory public inquiry–and as such they tell us more about major planning conflicts, cataclysmic changes, than about the inexorable summing of small development control approvals that in the end makes the greatest change to our surroundings. Interestingly, the state or its agents acts as developer in most of the cases selected, and for all the current criticism of closed government the arguments may be more fully exposed and debated than is always the case with major private developments.

The framework adopted is that of Alice Coleman's (1969) land use classification of three scapes: townscape, farmscape, and wildscape; and two fringes: rururban fringe and marginal fringe, to which the present author has added the hybrid coastal fringe. Alice Coleman views the three scapes as environments to be preserved and enhanced, the fringes as environments to reduce and replace. No such strictures apply in this chapter: the scapes and fringes shown in Fig. 5 simply appear to the author as a convenient and easily remembered way of classifying type localities each with characteristic development histories and contemporary development pressures. For those who wish to revive the neglected practice of reading topographic maps alongside place-bound text, the relevant Ordnance Survey 1:50,000 map sheets are given in each case study title.

Townscape: the London Docklands (sheet 177)

Docklands, an area of docks part derelict part working, stretches about 12 km astride the meandering River Thames downstream from Tower Bridge on the edge of the City of London. As demarcated in 1971 it comprised the riparian parts of five (Labour) London boroughs (named on Fig. 6), and in 1971 was the home of 55,000 people, 24,000 of whom were also among the 58,000 people then employed there. In 1971 the Conservative Environment Secretary, Peter Walker, announced in Parliament that an urgent and comprehensive study of the potential for rebuilding the London 'Docklands' would be undertaken by consultants. They were to have particular regard for measures for improving the quality of the environment for those presently living there, and five phased (over the period 1978–91) and costed options (some £670–950m. of public and private investment at 1971 prices) for restructuring the area were presented in 1973.

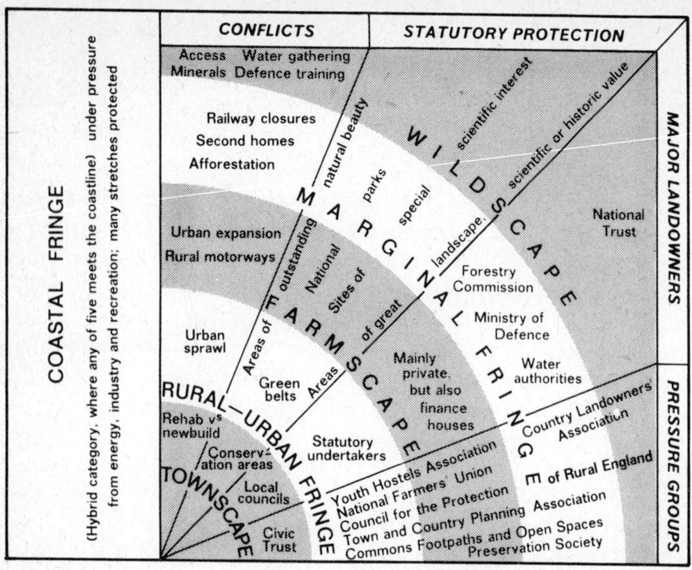

Fig. 5 Characteristics of scapes and fringes in the Alice Coleman typology. *After* A. Coleman (1969).

Peter Walker was well aware of the development opportunity afforded by the closure between 1967 and 1970 of the East India, London and St. Katharine, and Surrey Commercial docks. But the five boroughs and the newly-elected Labour GLC rejected all five options, declaring them to be unresponsive to local needs. Later in 1973 the (Conservative) national government acceded to the establishment of a Docklands Joint Committee (DJC) comprising politicians from the GLC and the boroughs, and government appointees, in three equal parts. During 1975 the new Docklands Development Team of planners produced thematic reports on topics such as housing, industry, and transport in order to elicit local residents' and workers' views.

The resulting *London Docklands strategic plan* (1976), approved by the DJC, sought 'to use the opportunity provided by large areas of London's Dockland becoming available to redress the housing, social, environmental, employment/economic and communications deficiencies of the Docklands area and the parent boroughs, and thereby, to provide the freedom for similar improvements throughout East and Inner London'. Contrary to the fashion prevailing in the mid-1970s for flexible frameworks and malleable plans, the strategy presented an unusually firm picture of redeveloped Docklands in 1997. Such an end-state master plan, although belonging to a species discredited elsewhere, was no doubt seen by the commissioning DJC as a statement of firm resolve; a blast to central government that they would brook nothing

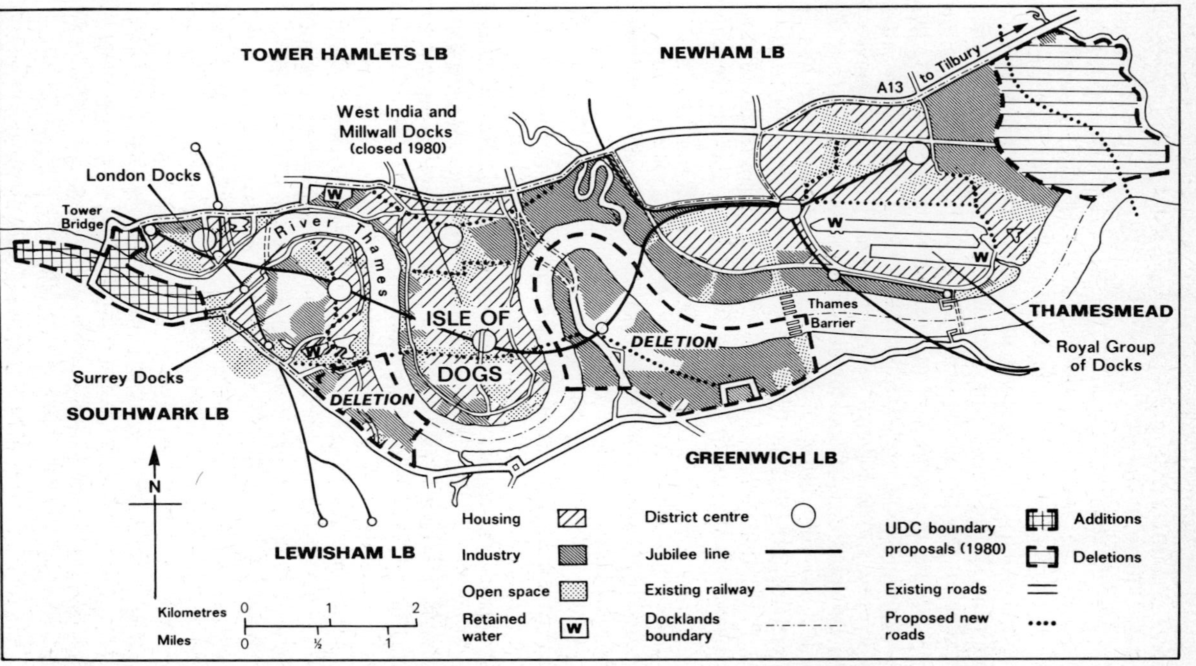

Fig. 6 London Docklands strategic plan 1976, showing possible structure when development complete (1997?), and the London Docklands Development Corporation boundary as first proposed in 1980 and approved in 1981.
Source: Docklands Joint Committee (1976); DoE letter dated 29 Oct. 1980.

but total commitment and the necessary financial support.

But neither of the two faces of central government–Parliament of government and opposition at Westminster, and the controlling party and civil servants in Whitehall–has matched mildly supportive rhetoric with cash for all the listed ingredients. The reasons are clear. Since the mid-1970s there has been ever-tighter limitation of public expenditure by both major political parties when in office. It has not been the time for expansive public works gestures such as a Docklands extension of the Jubilee line. Further, MPs from constituencies outside London have been critical of the Docklands proposals as further evidence of the metropolis spawning grandiose projects and pleading for special attention at a time of severe recession in the traditional industries of more peripheral regions. The regional policy implications of Docklands redevelopment were one of the three main issues investigated by the environment sub-committee of the House of Commons Expenditure Committee (HC 348, Session 1974-5; see further evidence in HC 269, 1978-9). MPs supported policies for occupational retraining rather than the rezoning Docklands as an assisted area in the government's regional policy. They also accepted that the rather unwieldy DJC should continue to supervise Docklands rebuilding, mainly because it was already there, and called on the DoE to indicate the likely range and phasing of public expenditure.

The strategic plan of 1976 had sought a 'minimal switch of national resources' in Docklands' favour–'of the order of 2 per cent of the government's planned local authority capital expenditure on housing and transport'. This request countered the Environment Secretary's reply to the MPs which emphasized that Docklands developments would simply be eligible for the normal forms of government support (Cmnd. 6193, 1975). But after the 1977-8 inner cities' statements and legislation the same Labour government was to introduce a 'partnership' committee between central government, GLC, and Docklands boroughs, and also to offer an increased urban programme funding for Docklands.

By 1979 public spending in the operational programme 1978-82 already showed a shortfall, and the strategic plan was being reviewed. Terms for the release of many vacant sites–Surrey Docks included–had not been agreed with private developers, and the incoming Conservative government spied 'a need for a single-minded determination not possible for the local authorities concerned with their much broader responsibilities'. So, for the redevelopment of docklands in London *and* in Liverpool, urban development corporations were the new preferred administrative structure. Operating from 1981, they have powers of planning, of land assembly and its disposal for industrial and commercial development in the private sector, of promoting environmental improvement, and of providing infrastructure and housing. Health, education, and social services remain locally controlled. Local boroughs and the Labour parliamentary opposition see these development corporation proposals as extra-territorial political dictatorship, unresponsive to local desires and conditions. For its part, the GLC expressed the view that Docklands progress had been inhibited more by lack of access to land, powers, and finance than by organizational difficulties, and that in any case the GLC (as Sir Frank Marshall (1978) had noted) saw itself, rather than any new tier of superimposed government, as being best fitted to exert strategic influence on docklands. But in 1981, shortly before being voted out of office, the Conservative GLC withdrew its objection to the draft parliamentary order creating the London Docklands Development Corporation. With other petitioners (the boroughs affected, tenants' associations, trades councils, and private developers), they had forced a lengthy hearing before a House of Lords select committee, which eventually found in the government's favour (HL 198, 1980–1) and recommended the creation of the LDDC within almost the exact boundaries suggested in 1980 (Fig. 6).

While these several debates, skirmishes, even open hostilities have been going on the derelict 'near east' docks have been largely conserved and redeveloped (the small St. Katharine's Dock), or at least sold off with joint public and private investment agreed (the larger London Docks and the Surrey Docks). But for many people living in the area the quality of their environment has not improved; parts may have remained the same, larger areas have deteriorated as widespread redundancies have been made in the docks, in ship repair, stevedoring, the laying of telecommunications cables, and food processing (see Community Development Project, 1977). Would a more vigorous and selfish thrust by each of the five boroughs have led to faster and less contentious redevelopment? Or would near east (i.e. near the City of London) Tower Hamlets and Southwark have prospered at the expense of far east, ill-drained Newham with its gargantuan, enclosed Royal docks (closed 1981)? As the leaders of the Docklands boroughs pointed out in their riposte against an urban development corporation (*Local democracy works*, 1979), claims that nothing had happened in Docklands, that the private sector had been discriminated against, and that large areas of land were readily available for disposal to developers, were largely mythical. Unfortunately, bursts of plans in 1973 and 1976, a reorientation in 1981–2, and successive bouts of public consultation have simply served to raise local expectations without raising local appreciation of the inevitably long lead times expended in making derelict dock and industrial sites suitable for redevelopment, and in procuring government and private funds–and even in recruiting people with the necessary skills.

Rururban fringe: the Hackney to M11 Link Road (sheet 177)

Trunk road and motorway inquiries take place under the Highways Acts 1959, 1971, and 1980 not the Town and Country Planning Acts, yet they are such an important and symbolically potent aspect of public sector spending that one scheme has been chosen to illustrate the geopolitical minefields on the rural-urban ('rururban') fringe. When motorways first appeared in Britain–the Preston bypass was the prototype in 1958–they were almost universally claimed to be a good thing. Motorway proposals now bring two opposed lobbies into public gaze: the British Road Federation, road hauliers, road contractors, and the like point to the impediment of congested historical towns crossed by heavy traffic, and of single-carriageway, multi-purpose trunk roads in rural areas. They advocate the segregation of traffic through the building of motorways as a means of improving road safety and the haulage industry's, and hence the nation's, economic efficiency. They are opposed by battle-bruised but still proud anti-motorway protesters such as John Tyme (1978). He has used the motorway inquiry as a laboratory for testing his formula that 'truth + courage + numbers = invincibility'.

London's politicians are now in the synthesis phase of the motorway dialectic. The thesis in the mid-1960s was that a newly constructed primary–i.e. motorway-standard–urban network of three 'ringways' and connecting radial routes, totalling about 500 km and displacing 50,000 people or so, would satisfy the then projected demand for movement in the 1980s. Such construction, costing about £1,100m. at 1970 prices, would have been augmented by an improved secondary network of some 1,600 km of existing roads, costing another £500m. Critics such as J. M. Thomson (1969) asked, amongst other things, where *public* transport fitted into the land use transportation planners' flow charts which led simply to road building. The antithesis, as expounded by the GLC's Labour politicians 1973–7, elected partly on a cry of 'No roads!', was the abandonment of most of the road proposals, and the removal of 'safeguarding' from many intended road corridors (Hart, 1976). The Conservative GLC (elected 1977) and national governments (elected 1979) came to point to growing road congestion in a metropolis that is almost entirely untouched by motorway construction, at least in the congested central commercial area and the surrounding inner city.

North-east London

Physical development in north-east London, most of which until the GLC was formed in 1965 was metropolitan Essex, has long been retarded by two barriers: the River Lea and Epping Forest. So we reach the urban fringe, here arrested by the metropolitan green belt, more quickly than in other quadrants. Furthermore Epping Forest's 2,300 ha, dedicated to the public as an open space 'for all time' after an Act of 1878, brings the forest commoners' grazing cattle and mercifully unkempt leafy glades within 10 km of the City of London. In 1973 a public consultation document showed four possible routes for a link road between two schemes in construction: the East Cross Route at Hackney and the M11 at Woodford (Fig. 7). In 1974 the Transport Minister announced

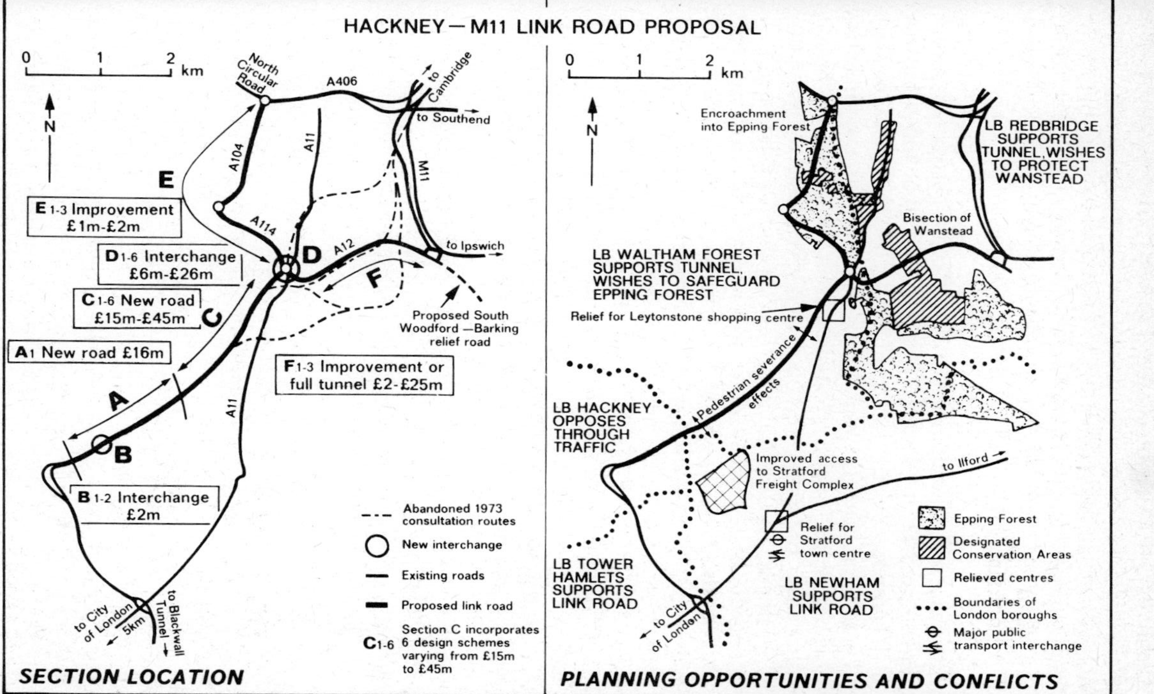

Fig. 7 Hackney to M11 Link Road: section selected for analysis and planning considerations. *Source*: Eastern Road Construction Unit (1979), figs. 2.2 and 5.1; table 7.1. (*Crown Copyright*) (The 1981 preferred scheme omitted section E.)

his preferred answer: a road from Hackney (B) to the Green Man (D), Cambridge Park (F) improvement, and widening of the A104/A114 sections. As a means of pre-empting many of the anticipated local government objections, a novel joint working party was established in 1976 comprising DTp and its Eastern Road Construction Unit officials, DoE and GLC planners, technical staff from the three London boroughs of Hackney, Redbridge, and Waltham Forest, and the DTp's consultants, Atkins Planning.

The working party's methods (Eastern Road Construction Unit, 1979) are here summarized because they are likely to be followed elsewhere in the country in the 1980s. The minister's 1974 outline was worked up as a 'balanced network strategy' so that the proposed link road would not simply pass on congestion from one bottleneck to another. Altogether the joint working party gave labels to forty-one objectives, national, London, and local, that the link road should satisfy (or at least approach). Hackney borough's principal objective, however, was to oppose the road on the grounds that more through traffic would be funnelled on to Hackney's already inadequate network. Using a low traffic growth assumption, morning peak-hour travel forecasts were made for 1985, the likely opening date, and 2001–the 'design year'. The capital costs, planning opportunities, and environmental impact of the several alternative schemes within each section were assessed (Table 3). At a later stage six sample composite schemes for the full link were assembled: one low cost (£41.8m.), three medium cost, and two high cost (£115m. maximum). Like the individual schemes they were compared for the capital cost, planning opportunities, and environmental impact, and gauged against the initial objectives.

In most road schemes, this urban link included, a cost-benefit analysis program calculates the Net Present Value (NPV) of each composite scheme comapred with the always present 'do nothing' alternative. The discounted costs (of construction, land purchase, and compensation) are subtracted from the discounted benefits (principally estimated savings of time and vehicle operating costs, although notional values can be given to accident reduction). In the link road the NPV/Cost ratio varies from +0.79 for the low cost variant to –0.33 for the highest cost tunnel scheme advocated by two local architects, J. Goldsmith and M. Lister. A negative value for the NPV/C ratio implies that a scheme could not be justified on economic grounds: overwhelming environmental and planning gains would have to be demonstrated to convince the Treasury and Environment and Transport Secretaries of its desirability. As Fig. 7 suggests, an expensive tunnel scheme would minimize pedestrian severance, noise, and visual intrusion along the Cambridge Park section which bisects the attractive residential neighbourhood of Wanstead; a local Link Road Action Group has publicized the merits of the unofficial Goldsmith–Lister scheme.

TABLE 3 *Hackney to M11 Link Road; summary of capital costs, benefits, planning opportunities, and environmental impact*

	Low cost	Medium cost			High cost	
Composite scheme	1	2	3	4	5	Lister/ Goldsmith*
Economic evaluation (Link Road only variant)						
capital cost (Jan. 1978 prices £m.)						
— construction	35.0	41.7	50.2	58.8	72.5	107.6
— land and property	6.8	6.9	6.9	6.9	7.1	7.5
total cost	41.8	48.6	57.1	65.9	79.0	115.1
total discounted to 1976 (C)	21.4	24.8	28.6	32.9	38.8	56.4
total discounted benefits (B)	38.2	38.2	37.5	37.5	36.8	37.7
Net Present Value (B–C)	16.8	13.4	8.9	4.6	–2.0	–18.7
NPV/C ratio (B–C)/(C)	0.79	0.54	0.31	0.14	–0.05	–0.33
Planning opportunities and environmental impact						
All schemes relieve Leytonstone High Road shopping centre						
All schemes reduce Stratford traffic by about 25%						
housing demotion	343	353	350	365	369	392
dwellings qualifying for double glazing	247	229	229	203	167	13
potential new homes at 65/ha	15	15	15	0	203	0
new open space (ha)	4.4	4.1	3.8	5.4	6.3	18.4*
excavated material for removal '000m^3	267	447	511	616	675	929
approx. construction period (years)	2½	2½	3	3	3½	3½

* Long tunnel scheme with linear park above.
Source: Eastern Road Construction Unit (1979), tables 7.3–7.6.
Note: The 1981 preferred scheme incorporated a 300m tunnel at Wanstead.

Now that the national strategic trunk road network of about 11,000 km is largely complete, at least in most rural areas, increasing attention will be given to deciding where, how and when to improve heavily-trafficked sections and junctions in and around urban areas, such as the link here described. The current methods of assembling and assessing trunk road proposals, including traffic forecasting and economic and environmental evaluation, have been examined by Sir George Leitch's (1977) Advisory Committee on Trunk Road Assessment (see also Lassière, 1976). A twenty-three-stage progress from identifying the need for a road to opening it is charted by Leitch (his Table 1.3); as an appendix to the White Paper *Policy for roads: England 1978* (Cmnd. 7132, 1978) showed, ten years is the shortest preparation period for a typical scheme.

In many road schemes fifteen years or more will lapse while the sequence unfolds and refolds. Mindful of several road inquiries notorious for the protesters' disruptive tactics–M25, M40, Aire Valley, Archway in London–the Departments of Environment and of Transport announced measures for improving the flow of information for inquiry objectors (*Report on the review of highway inquiry procedures*, Cmnd. 7133, 1978). Beesley and Kettle (1979) see continuing conflict even within the fully exposed Leitch comprehensive appraisal framework, and so propose the experimental creation of a lay jury of non-affected parties to pronounce on the relative merits of the distribution effects of gains and losses associated with competing proposed routes.

Farmscape surrendered: Milton Keynes new city (sheet 152)

Farmscape in Alice Coleman's framework should remain just that: lowland areas best suited to agricultural production. Some of the unwelcome visual consequences of technological change on the farm have been described by Westmacott and Worthington (1974), and debated by the Countryside Commission (*Discussion Paper* 76A, 1974; CCP 102, 1977). However, by alighting on Milton Keynes new city we can observe how rolling fields are still transformed into rows of houses.

Milton Keynes was designated as a new town in 1967, but with a projected increase (then) from a base population of 40,000 in Bletchley, Wolverton, and Stony Stratford to 250,000 it should really be dubbed a 'new city'. By the proposed scale of development and incorporation of existing towns it is typical of the 'third generation' of British new towns. By the late 1960s it had become desirable to graft London overspill on to significant existing towns (Northampton 133,000; Peterborough 81,000; Bletchley itself 30,000), and to use new town designation as a device to combine expansion with unmixing the jumbled inheritance of the industrial revolution, at the Central Lancashire New Town (base 235,000) and at Warrington (base 122,000).

Milton Keynes was conceived of in 1962 by county officials in Buckinghamshire and nourished by the regional population growth anticipated in the Ministry of Housing and Local Government's *South East study 1961-1981* of 1964, and the South East Economic Planning Councils's *Strategy for the South East* of 1967. A draft designation order was followed by a public inquiry in 1966-7, and the master plan was ready two years after the appointment of the Milton Keynes Development Corporation in 1967. Non-elected new town development corporations possess effective planning powers because they can acquire land by compulsory purchase and can expect to deploy a sizeable budget to build on generally greenfield sites according to an approved master plan. Milton Keynes Development Corporation's master plan (1970) shows how and where some 150,000 newcomers could be accommodated, employed, serviced, and entertained by the 1990s on a site of 8,900 ha. The consultants, Llewelyn-Davies, Weeks, Forestier-Walker and Bor, had been most susceptible to recent advances in American city planning, and through half-closed eyes the 1 km^2 grid of roads laid out south-west of the M1 and astride the A5 and London-Glasgow main-line railway does resemble Los Angeles.

The grid, a form found in the most ancient of cities in the Middle East, here encloses neighbourhoods with about 5,000 residents, and also containing mixed industrial, commercial, and social uses. Traffic-generating land uses are deliberately scattered about the city so that the road network is more evenly loaded than happens in, say, Stevenage, where the industrial area is separated from the town by the railway. In Milton Keynes shops and schools are mainly found at crossing points between neighbourhoods.

The master plan grows out of the assumption that future inhabitants must have the greatest possible choice of how and where to live. Four categories of environmental control were proposed. Detailed design briefs would safeguard areas of special importance, such as around existing village nuclei. In a second group of areas control would be minimal, subject only to safety, sanitation, and access. A third group would comprise sites for unsightly and noisy activities, and in the fourth 'remainder' category the corporation 'would not discourage idiosyncratic taste'.

Obviously the free-wheeling plan has attracted much attention: the journal *Architectural Design* carried the views of proponents and opponents (issues 6, 1973; 8 and 10, 1974; 1 and 3, 1975). A decade on, it is the equally emphasized *social* development programme, designed to complement the physical and economic plans, that interests many visitors. R. Cowan (1978) has described innovations in new towns, including Milton Keynes. Here in 'MK' we find a neighbourhood care programme that provides visits by officials and volunteers to all new families. A person labelled the 'job creator' scouts out innovation technologies, new products, and new young enterprises that might settle in the city. Someone else finds jobs for the disabled. Over 100 traditional leisure technologies and skills from knitting to yoga are demonstrated by volunteers in homes or community workshops. Cheap used furniture is collected, repaired, and reallocated. You need not wait at a windswept bus stop–Dial-a-Bus brings the bus to your doorstep and deposits you exactly where you want to get off. Architects find out from 'residential design feedback' surveys what went wrong between drawing board and inhabitation; difficulties of settling in and service delivery are gauged by an independent social survey. Underground services–gas, water, electricity, even community cablevision–sensibly but unusually share a common trench. Mindful also of Nan Fairbrother's deserved jibes (1970) about councils' 'fitted carpet complexes'–an obsession with a close-mown grass and concrete jig-saw filling all urban interstices–the survey of all existing trees and hedgerows in Milton

Keynes shows species, age, dimension, health, life expectancy, and importance.

And if one institution typifies this brave experiment of sensitive software in flexible hardware, it is the Open University established in 1969. A combination of high technology (television) with low (letter box); a guiding philosophy of do-it-yourself-with-a-little-help-from-us for those reading for degrees at home; accommodation in new huts and a restored country house. So Milton Keynes, in addition to attracting an energetic team of architects, planners, and surveyors, has also attracted other workers excited by developing new technologies. This particular version of applied futurology would appear to work reasonably well.

Marginal fringe: Exmoor national park (sheets 180 and 181)

Exmoor is well described by its name. The River Exe rises in the heart of heather-clad or grass moorlands often attaining elevations of 500 m, and later etches a deep valley or coombe along its southerly course from Somerset into Devon. The combination of remoteness, wild plateau, and cultivated valley bottoms led to the designation of Exmoor as a national park in 1954. Apart from the Pembrokeshire coast park it is the smallest in England and Wales (686 km^2; the Lake District is largest with 2,243 km^2). In 1968 the Exmoor National Park committee selected 17,000 ha of unimproved moorland–about 25 per cent of the total park area–for designation as 'Critical Amenity Area' (CAA) within which it was hoped to preserve the existing moorland landscape.

Now it so happens that almost the entire CAA qualifies for preferential hill cow and hill sheep grant aid under EEC directive 73/268, and that about two-thirds of the hill land within the CAA is thought to be capable of agricultural improvement. A conflict therefore arises between local farmers–who may wish to take up grants to drain, ditch, fence, plough, lime, and grass the moorland, and so stock it with higher densities of hardy breeding ewes and cattle–and those who wish to preserve the presently familiar Exmoor landscape. Both groups are represented on the national park committee of Somerset County Council. Fourteen members are councillors elected to the four constituent county and district councils. Many of them are guided by Section 37 of the Countryside Act 1968 that requires ministers and local authorities to have 'due regard to the needs of agriculture and forestry and to the economic and social interests of rural areas'. In contrast, the seven appointed by the Environment Secretary may be more mindful of Section 11 which refers to the 'desirability of conserving the natural beauty and amenity of the countryside'. The Sandford national park policy review committee (1974) had called for better co-ordination between agricultural and environmental policies, although the 1979 agriculture White Paper (Cmnd. 7458) appeared almost entirely preoccupied with production and distribution costs in a period of high inflation and in the context of EEC policy-making.

Controversy over moorland reclamation in Exmoor has become so intense in recent years that in April 1977 the Environment Secretary and Agriculture Minister asked Lord Porchester to assess the moorland changes, consider how the various interests might find a balance, and make recommendations. The Porchester report (1977) describes how he held local hearings and received written evidence. A rate of loss of moorland in Exmoor of between 400 and 600 ha a year was estimated for 1968–77, although a parliamentary question (23 Mar. 1977) elicited the reply of about 260 ha of CAA improved with grant aid in the preceding five years. Rather more confidently, it was shown from air photographs that between 1947 and 1976 some 4,850 ha of moorland out of the park total of 23,900 ha had been lost: 20 per cent to woodland, 80 per cent to agricultural conversion or improvement.

Not all of the remaining moorland within and even outside the CAA is at risk. The National Trust owns about 22 per cent of the CAA, and other public bodies another 7 per cent, so some 4,800 ha are unlikely to be disposed of or improved. Rights of commoning are also exercised over some of the publicly owned land; this is an additional safeguard against improvement. If all of Exmoor's improveable land were improved, then the Agriculture Ministry's estimate of the annual gain to UK agricultural output would be 708 tonnes of mutton and lamb (0.27 per cent), 109,000 kg of wool (0.2 per cent), and 610 tonnes of beef and veal (0.05 per cent). But the benefit to the individual farmer can be considerable, especially when it is remembered that many hill and upland farmers derive more than half their income from subsidies of various sorts.

Lord Porchester investigated the prevailing system of 'gentleman's agreements' between the park authority, National Farmers' Union, Country Landowners' Association, and Ministry of Agriculture whereby six months' notice is given to the authority by any farmer intending to reclaim moorland within the CAA. All parties to this method of agreement, together with the Royal Institute of Chartered Surveyors, favoured the retention of the voluntary principle, and opposed supplementary compulsory powers. But a minority of national park committee members believed that the voluntary principle had failed. Lord Porchester proposed technical and procedural solutions to the impasse. First the park authority should survey moor and heath and define anew particular tracts of land whose appearance the authority wanted to see conserved, so far as possible, 'for all time'. The Agricultural Ministry's Agricultural Development and Advisory Service (ADAS) would discourage farmers seeking grant aid for reclamation in these areas, and presumably suggest alternative methods of supplementing farm income, say by erecting buildings for in-wintering stock, or by tourism. If an ADAS recommendation against grant aiding was rejected by the farmer, the authority should then be empowered to serve a 'moorland conservation order'. Such an order would allow the farmer to receive financial compensation for the surrender of the right to convert moorland, and the existing vegetation cover would be preserved.

Legislation which included the moorland conservation order fell when Parliament was prorogued in May 1979, but was accepted by the succeeding administration for inclusion in their own new Wildlife and Countryside Bill. Parts of other national parks have also been much altered by the ploughing-up of moorland, for example the North York Moors (Statham, 1972), and even the Peak District where Parry (1977) has used Ordnance Survey maps and air photographs to define the historical moorland core, fluctuating fringe, and improved farmland.

Changing agricultural technology and economics are no less destructive of familiar lowland rural landscapes. The Countryside Commission sponsored a report by Westmacott and Worthington (1974) on new agricultural landscapes in type localities. Their brief was to study 'how agricultural improvement can be carried out efficiently but in such a way as to create new landscapes no less interesting than those destroyed in the process'. Landscape protection and nature conservation issues have also been considered by semi-government bodies (e.g. Nature Conservancy Council, 1977; the Strutt Advisory Committee for Agriculture and Horticulture, 1978; and the Countryside Review Committee, 1976 and 1979), and independently of government (MacEwan, 1976; Davidson and Lloyd, 1977). Countryside planning matters in general are examined by Cherry (1976), Davidson and Wibberley (1977), and Gilg (1979).

Wildscape: Cow Green Reservoir (sheet 91)

Cow Green, a treeless and uninhabited fell on the north bank of the upper reaches of the River Tees, just above Caldron Snout and between the Moor House and Teesdale national nature reserves, achieved notoriety in 1966 when it gave its name to a bitterly opposed reservoir scheme. The values of pure scientists, fearful for arctic-alpine plant communities on Widdybank Fell that had survived since the ice retreat 10,000–15,000 years ago, were in direct conflict with those of applied scientists working for Imperial Chemical Industries on Teesside, and the Tees Valley and Cleveland Water Board, who wanted increased water supplies for ICI's new nitrogenous fertilizer plants. Parliamentary committees in both Houses, but principally in the House of Lords, were responsible for the final adjudication. That the conservationists 'lost' can be seen at the 572 m-long dam completed in 1970 which now contains a reservoir of 40.8 million m^3 capacity (Kennard and Reader, 1975).

In 1964 ICI asked the Water Board to double its clean water supplies from 25 to 50 million gallons per day. Cow Green was one of seventeen possible sites considered, and as a result of recent geotechnical and river regulation advances was now preferred; its hydrological attraction had been longer evident. The Water Board promoted the Tees Valley and Cleveland Water Bill in 1965. Ecologists, alarmed by the prospect of the drowning of 7 ha of Cow Green, were even more horrified at the thought of how construction and subsequent impounding and water-table changes could affect the fragile arctic–alpine flora on the adjacent Widdybank and Cronkley Fells. This unique British community with its refuge of rare and unique species has been fully described by Pigott (1956). At a meeting of the Teesdale Defence Committee Dr Max Walters of the Cambridge University herbarium said that 'In terms of pure botanical science alone, Upper Teesdale has revealed its secrets in an impressive way. To destroy this open-air laboratory should be as unthinkable to the nation as would be a similar sacrifice of Westminster Abbey or Ely Cathedral.'

But the debate that followed in the House of Lords and select committee hearing raised questions about hypothetical jobs and exports, which curiously always seem more tangible than the observable spring sandwort (*Minuartia stricta*) or the Teesdale violet (*Viola rupestris*). That ICI was buying water at 1*s.* 1*d.* (5½p) per thousand gallons compared with 3*s.* (15p) national average led Lord Molson to suggest that ICI had ample opportunity to pay a higher price for a reservoir further downstream at Middleton in Teesdale. Here, however, more farmland of higher quality would have been inundated. But all other sites and methods were rejected. The parliamentary battle is described by Gregory (1971 and 1975).

Subsequent events give rise to a measure of relief but also to lingering dismay. Relief derives from surveys of flora, and more especially invertebrate fauna in the reservoir basin and below the dam. In respect of the fauna, the Freshwater Biological Association's research into the impact of impoundment completed in 1978 shows an increase in the number and biomass of certain taxa, but generally not at the expense of the previous fauna (*NERC report for 1977–78*, HC 678, 1978). Lingering dismay derives from the fact that the water industry in England and Wales was reorganized by the Water Act 1973. Water supply and treatment were henceforward entrusted to nine regional water authorities, and the increase in scale of operations has been mirrored by a national view of demand and of ways of meeting it. Since April 1974, the Tees Valley and Cleveland Water Board has been part of the Tees Division of the Northumbrian Water Authority. Would ICI now expect the local Tees catchment to satisfy its demand for water, or could a regional pipeline transfer water from the much larger Kielder reservoir scheme approved in 1975? And are parliamentary debates and hearings, limited to particular sites held in front of parliamentarians largely untutored in scientific affairs, an adequate method for resolving conflicts such as Cow Green?

Coastal fringe: a Windscale nuclear reprocessing plant (sheet 89)

Windscale (1977) ranks with the Roskill Commission (1968–70) and Belvoir (1979–80) as one of the three great planning debates in Britain in the 1970s. Speaking in the 'Windscale (Special Development Order)' debate in the House of Commons on 15 May 1978 (HC *Debates*, cols. 111–82 for that day), Mr Anthony Wedgwood Benn said that the debate was 'not a theological dispute about the intrinsic merit of nuclear power. We are talking about electricity and how to get it.' To him, the debate was about two known risks: nuclear reprocessing, and an anticipated national energy shortage arising from the country's reliance on non-nuclear sources. Other MPs were more interested in the prospect of an agreement with Japan to receive a sizeable fee for reprocessing their waste.

Windscale, on the remote Cumbrian coastal fringe at Sellafield, within 2 km of the western flank of the Lake District National Park, happens to be British Nuclear Fuel Ltd.'s (BNFL) plant for reprocessing, cooling, and storing spent fuel from nuclear reactors. (Across the River Calder lies Calder Hall, Britain's first civil nuclear power station, which became operational in 1956.) To the now growing and amalgamating 'anti-nuke' lobby, Windscale is synonymous with a protracted public inquiry into an application made by BNFL on 1 March 1977 to develop a thermal oxide reprocessing plant (THORP) at Windscale. BNFL is a wholly-owned subsidiary of the state Atomic Energy Authority.

For this chapter Windscale can be viewed in three ways: in terms of the broad issues of nuclear power, of how a public inquiry came to be called into an issue that few MPs in Cabinet or in Parliament wanted to be made public, and of a catalogue of the proclivities of nuclear installation designers for coastal sites. Taking these in reverse order, we notice that apart from five inland research locations, two Severn estuary installations, and Trawsfynydd in North Wales, the eleven presently licensed nuclear sites in the UK are on generally sparsely-populated sections of the coast. Nuclear power stations, like coal-burning stations, release heat to drive steam turbines and so require more cooling water than Britain's short shallow rivers can supply and reabsorb. By being remote, the chance of using the hot water for neighbourhood heating is lost, of course; but in their sixth report, *Nuclear power and the environment* (Flowers, 1976) the Royal Commission on Environmental Pollution favoured 'near-urban' sites, as at Hartlepool and Heysham, where waste heat can be harnessed. And given the need to safeguard the coastline and to reduce runs of unsightly overhead power lines, nuclear sites are likely to be closer to major cities in the future.

Given the hostility of central government to an inquiry, as reported by Breach (1978) and Bugler (1978)–of Defence, Energy, Foreign and Commonwealth Office, Treasury, and Environment departmental interests, and the reported reluctance of the environment secretary to usurp the statutory powers of the more recently-formed Cumbria County Council–it is remarkable that a public inquiry was held. The county planning committee, although mindful of widespread local support for the BNFL proposal, had declared the application to be a departure from the county structure plan, and the committee chairman had called for a public inquiry in a letter to *The Times* rather than direct to the minister. Bugler reports that after a second attempt, the Cabinet allowed Peter Shore, then Environment Secretary, to announce a public inquiry. The Hon. Mr Justice Parker was appointed inspector, aided by two eminent technical assessors.

Inspectors' rules allow relevant issues–possibly as specified by the ministry–to be identified at the outset. Here, these included implications for the safety of the public, for other (unspecified) aspects of the national interest, and for the environment; the area's amenities; local employment and services; and the effects of additional traffic movements by road and rail. The 100-day inquiry generated 1,500 documents, many of book length, and five objectors' films. Begetters and objectors (e.g. Town and Country Planning Association, 1978) gave evidence and cross-examined on issues of energy forecasts, state security and terrorist threats, special constabularies, and radiation hazards. Mr Justice Parker had posed three questions at the outset. Should oxide fuel from UK reactors be reprocessed in this country at all, whether at Windscale or elsewhere? If yes, should it be at Windscale? If yes again, should the plant be about double the estimated size required to handle UK fuels, and its spare capacity used for reprocessing foreign fuels? After hearing–and, according to seventeen objectors writing to *The Times*, also misunderstanding, misrepresenting, distorting, or ignoring, the evidence–Mr Justice Parker's report (1978) answered, respectively, yes and without delay, yes, and yes, to the three questions. His assessors agreed.

By actually refusing the application, but announcing (HC *Debates*, 6 Mar. 1978, cols. 981-91) that he would authorize the development subject to the conditions recommended by the inspector, Peter Shore paved the way for a wider parliamentary debate. In fact two debates followed. In the first (HC *Debates*, 22 Mar. 1978, cols. 1537-676) after publication of the Parker report, much of the six and a half hours was taken up by the Foreign Secretary's assurances on nuclear proliferation, bearing in mind that Japan was not a signatory to the international treaty and that President Carter had strong views. The second (HC *Debates*, 15 May 1978, cols. 111-82) was precipitated by the special development order. Before it comfortably passed the House the Liberal leader, David Steel, showed how issues raised at the Windscale planning inquiry were fundamental to the hazards of life and enjoyment of civil liberties for generations to come (see also Flood and Grove-White, 1976). Once the decision to proceed was taken it would be difficult to go back to a less nuclear economy, he thought. Public opinion is often distrustful of experts, but at Windscale it was the *opponents* who were presented as 'cranks or political misfits'. We needed further evidence into the safety and security of nuclear materials on site and in transit, and of waste storage. And finally, said Mr Steel, if we go ahead we shall be giving an international lead in the wrong direction.

Doubtless the anti-nuclear lobby (see CIS, 1978; Croall and Sempler, 1978), already well organized in the USA and in mainland Europe, will grow in Britain to oppose the post-1979 Conservative government's espousal of the nuclear option. In 1976 the Flowers Royal Commission reported that the current 'official' energy strategy forecast 60 per cent penetration of the UK energy market in the year 2025 by electricity, compared with 13 per cent in 1975. Three-quarters of the installed capacity would be nuclear. Under a largely coal alternative electricity's market share of 13 per cent could be constrained to 19 per cent by 2025 in an alternative energy strategy. By accepting Mr Justice Parker's Windscale answers about infill plant on a particular coastal nuclear site, successive governments may have foreclosed on this latter low nuclear option (see also Pearce *et al.*, 1979).

Seascape?

In a few years' time, given the continuing exploitation of the continental shelf around these islands, it may be sensible to talk of a *seascape* category of landscape with policy implications. Certainly the biological, economic, and militaristic significance of the several seas around our shores is not in doubt. The control of licensing, locating, policing, regulating, surveying, and taxing offshore activities is divided among many national and international agencies. Governments, their lawyers, and implicated domestic agencies will doubtless engage in unending struggle for larger spheres of control. And the greater the developments off shore, the greater the on shore developments at the coast to service them.

Further reading

Theories, practices and polemics in land use change are investigated by, respectively:

D. Rhind and R. Hudson (1980) *Land use* (Methuen).

M. Blacksell and A. W. Gilg (1981) *The countryside: planning and change* (Allen & Unwin).

M. Shoard (1980) *Theft of the countryside* (Maurice Temple Smith).

6 The planning process reviewed

Accounting for the relative 'success' or 'failure' of published 'plans' is avowedly difficult. The economic climate and social expectations of a country or even a region can change significantly during the nominal period of currency of a plan. Perhaps more to the point at a local level, planning staff may be promoted or relocated away from the plan that they devised; political priorities may swing significantly; key political chairmen may retire. Superimpose the reorganization of British local government 1973-5, and the shifts of emphasis and efflorescence of passing fashions in planning, and the difficulty of undertaking convincing 'hindsight evaluation' becomes apparent.

Critical evaluations and suggestions for improvement in planning are often made at the more leisurely planning conferences, for example the RTPI's annual Town and Country Planning Summer School. Distinguished planners are invited to give prestigious lectures, for example the 1972 Chichele lectures at Oxford by Sir Colin Buchanan published as *The state of Britain* (1973). Buchanan labels as significant 'planning' successes building a corruption-free planning machinery, curbing sprawl, clearing slums, implementing a brilliant new schools programme, new towns, national parks, clean air, control of advertisements, conservation measures, assisted areas, and so forth. But in the debit column he notes the 'general deterioration of the quality of life in inner urban areas', an inadequate marriage between land use and economic and social policies, housing shortage and polarity between the public and private sectors, continuing urban traffic problems and lack of transport integration, continuing noise and vehicle emissions, urban design failures, and planning delays.

Part of the difficulty of evaluating plans derives from the problems of measurement. Broad policies, detailed programmes, and individual projects within one sector, such as housing, where there is a mass of local authority data in addition to national surveys of construction, details of Housing Investment Programmes (HIP), and measures of occupation and facilities from the census of population, lend themselves to academic scrutiny. Housing policy in London, for example, is particularly well served, as the list of works cited in Young and Kramer (1978) testifies. Additionally, individual sectors may have more precisely defined targets or goals, and the regular receipt of government funds of the HIP or transport programme type for approved schemes, than is the case for development or structure plans that may in practice simply combine sectoral intentions and are not in themselves funded. The adoption of performance reviews in comprehensive community programmes (see Hambleton, 1978) should improve understanding of the pitfalls in implementing plans in respect of not meeting targets (spending and timetables).

Performance evidenced by land use patterns?

It is the lack of hard data that in part fuels the continuing and excitable debate about the significance of 'land losses' (if you are alarmed), 'transfers' or 'conversions' (if you are not) from agricultural to urban uses. Robin Best has been estimating rates of conversion for more than two decades, and shows that the rate of urbanization 1951-71, at about 15,000 ha per year in England and Wales, was lower than the rate of 19,500 ha per year in 1921-39 (Best, 1976). From about 10 per cent 'urban' at present, some 14 per cent of the land surface of England and Wales could be so occupied by the turn of the century. Alice Coleman expounds the conservationist approach, rather than the land budgeting through demand forecasting method. She hopes to alarm by extrapolation, stating that in respect of improved farmland (about two-thirds of the land area of England and Wales in 1963) 'the date of extinction is now estimated at 200 years hence or less' (Coleman, 1977). Certainly Lord Vernon has found the possibility frightening (HL *Debates*, 21 Mar. 1979, vol. 399, cols. 1201-34). But even if such extrapolation allows no flattening of the supposedly S-shaped curve for the growth in quantity of space per person within the home and within settlements, and neglects the remodelling of presently built-up areas, the evidence about land quality in Miss Coleman's second land use survey cannot be so lightly dismissed. Comparison of the first and second land utilization surveys in the 1930s and 1960s shows significant increases in the area covered by scrub and infested by bracken, in derelict and urban waste land, and in the fragmentation of formerly coherent farm units on the urban fringe. The few patches of Grade I agricultural land in Britain have likewise been eroded significantly. Miss Coleman would like to see a reduction of the area of her two buffering fringes, and a clear-cut allocation of land to appropriate townscape, farmscape, or wildscape functions. Her views are reinforced by the Land Decade Educational Council (1979) which would like to see all plan-making undertaken with the overriding goal of preserving farmland for agricultural production and expanding forestry. Such a view is fundamentally different from that (chapter 3 gives examples) in which planning seeks to accommodate the demands on land engendered by rising population numbers and increasing consumption of space for work and leisure activities.

Explanations: techniques, organization, social formation?

Planning's failures, as Buchanan's list indicates, include more than land use abuses and ambiguities. We might consider three aspects of the 'software' that brings the 'hardware' of physical investment into being: techniques, administrative organization, and ideology.

From the not unrelated advent of cheap and relatively easy-to-master data processing and numerate social sciences there emerged an 'urban modelling' school of researchers seeking more exact mathematical descriptions and predictions of the connections between population, employment, housing, services, and related patterns of trips and demands for space. But there seems to have been a persistent gulf between the increasing prowess of the theoretical system builders and the continuing inability of practising, politically responsive planners to control effectively the development of such 'system elements' on the ground. Nevertheless there is considerable merit in applying associated simulation and role-play techniques for educating planners, politicians, and public about the inter-connectedness of changes (see, for example, Taylor, 1971).

If a misplaced faith in numerical techniques is part of planning's failure to comprehend socially-determined change, then planners might also plead that they have been unfairly handicapped by inappropriate organizational structures and administrative boundaries. The Local Government Act 1972 that created counties and districts in England and Wales in 1974 also shared, and in some cases duplicated, development control powers among these two tiers of government. New planning teams have been created, using untried new techniques within, latterly, newly constituted authorities.

Many recently trained planners also have a radically divergent view of what they are doing compared with their older colleagues. Alice Coleman (1977) writes wryly that an article in a planning journal 'even took it for granted that the purpose of planning is to redistribute wealth. Caveat the Exchequer!' Yet approved development plans can most certainly accelerate rises or falls in land values according to what is zoned to locate, or to pass, where. To locate public 'goods' may also be to circumscribe the location of 'bads'. The thesis advanced by writers such as David Harvey (1973 and 1976) is that most actions undertaken in the name of planning, certainly in capitalist (and maybe in socialist?) economies have simply improved the quality of life of the already privileged, and further impoverished the surroundings of the poor. Peter Ambrose and Bob Colenutt (1975) emphasize the point that 'There can be no planning decision that provides *only* benefits and, moreover, provides them in equal proportions to all residents affected.' In a Marxian view the planner taking decisions becomes an agent of class repression; he helps to reproduce a built physical environment that expresses the social relations of capital.

David Eversley (1973), writing in part out of his experiences as chief strategic planner with the GLC, certainly felt that several 'radical' planners recruited to the GLC in the early 1970s were trying to subvert or sabotage the planning system. And with the entry of even more graduate social science geographers, sociologists, economists, and historians into planning jobs since Eversley wrote, it is not surprising that the texts currently generating most interest in many graduate planning schools are those of the 'new urban sociology' and its 'instrumentalist', 'managerialist', and 'structuralist' variants identified in the literature analysed, for example, by Peter Saunders (1979). In Cynthia Cockburn's analysis (1977) of the 'local state', community action is seen as a diversion: it points to deficiencies in the provision of goods and services, not to deficiencies in the dominant (capitalist) mode of production. John Dearlove (1979) likewise sees technocratic practices and the enlargement of councils as an attempt to remove political power from the working class.

Planning's future?

Professions are alert to criticism from outside their ranks. Ample evidence of this is to be found in a multi-disciplinary, working group discussion paper on *Planning and the future* (RTPI, 1976) which considered changing societal pressures and proposed a new approach to planning. The group's novel proposal that ten or fifteen years' evolutionary change should eventually be enshrined in legislation–custom inverted–has been scotched already by the present Conservative government's planning leglislation. Contrary to the working group's vision of a National Resource Planning Agency there is to be no national inventory of resource assets: the Wildlife and Countryside Act sees conservation in terms of protecting especially important natural habitats. Elsewhere detailed planning and aesthetic controls are to be relaxed (see DoE Circular 22/80). The chancellor's 1980 budget endorsed 'enterprise zones' as a means of revitalizing selected derelict sites (HC *Debates*, 26 Mar. 1980, cols. 1487-9; seven sites were listed in HC *Debates*, 29 July 1980, cols. 1312-13). Within the zones, building regulations and planning permissions are relaxed so long as developers conform to the overall design brief, and a total derating of industrial and commercial property is offered. In conception, if not in their industrial orientation, they resemble the anarchistic 'non-plan' approach floated in a *New Society* team polemic (Banham *et al.*, 1969).

In the prevailing mood of 'everything must pay its way in the world', social science research is not an activity highly regarded by government, and the Social Science Research Council (SSRC) has seen its budget reduced significantly. Its Planning Committee had already reviewed topics for priority and for partial relegation when assessing the merit of researchers' proposals for project support (SSRC, 1976). Topics for reduced concern included mathematical modelling, international comparisons outside Europe, and the impact of large projects.

Many inportant, researchable questions yet remained unanswered in the SSRC planning committee's view: what is the role of the Treasury, and of public involvement? How do planning 'standards' (housing density, playing field and playspace provision, retail floorspace, and so forth) relate to people's life-styles and aspirations? (The findings of broader 'quality of life' surveys are described by J. F. Hall, 1976.) How effective is special funding on priority areas rather than on individuals or families in need? What effect has planning had on employment and income, especially on the inner-city economy and its residents? Currently, although hardly in 1976, speculations are appearing about microprocessors and whether more of the fewer working people might be able to work at home.

The world's best land use planning system?

The 1947 Planning Act augmented land use planning in Britain by nationalizing development rights: owners could henceforward change the use of land and buildings only with permission. Land use changes in all parts of the country were soon to be approved or rejected by reference to a development plan tested by public inquiry and scrutinized by the planning ministry. With some justification this land use planning system was dubbed the best in the world by many commentators, who were as mindful of actions visible in the landscape as of flow charts and organizational structures. Increasingly the claim has a jingoistic ring. As we have seen, selective planning controls in Britain are being relaxed, formal regional strategy-making is in abeyance, and it becomes ever harder to discern what is happening to, or what is desired for, the *national* plannedscape. Furthermore, neighbours on mainland Europe have now refined their own planning systems. The consequences of following alternative directions of change in the Netherlands are clearly presented by their planning ministry and widely debated, not least in the national parliament.

Wide-ranging debates on regional and land use planning, nature conservation, participation, and local government effectiveness have long been common in the broadly-constituted Council of Europe. There is increasing evidence that the more exclusive and tightly structured EEC (see Commission paper COM (80)253 final) is also becoming alert to land use planning issues, whether because of common concern for safeguarding energy supplies, minimizing energy expenditure by alternative settlement and transport configurations, safeguarding vulnerable wildlife habitats, or minimizing international transfers of pollution. Word-pictures of anticipatory and more radical exploratory scenarios, based on currently discernible social and political trends, have been produced by the European Cultural Foundation's international study of *Europe 2000* (P. Hall, 1977). Similarly, but more briefly, five alternative futures for Britain were revealed in a *New Society* collection (17 Nov. 1977, 338 and 343–54); they form scenarios of the social and political context within which planning might operate, rather than describe planned physical futures. To contemplate where the *loci* of political power might reside in an incrementally or a cataclysmically transformed Britain is also to contemplate who might control funds for expanding and reconstructing the physical face of the nation.

Enduring questions

Although this volume is in a series entitled 'Theory and Practice in Geography', I have had little to say directly about geography, assuming that the reader would soon sense that my own view of geography comprehends how our everyday surroundings came to us in their present form and, more importantly, seeks to understand who is trying to change them, in what form and for whose benefit, and with what spatial outcome. Many geography undergraduates have later turned planners, or as academics have commanded the attention of planners (Willatts, 1971).

One would like to think that their concern for facilitating improvements in tomorrow's environment was shared by the 15 per cent or so of their former fellow students who preferred the teaching profession. To be sure, most of us have a view, possibly hazy, of a pleasanter land —which really means towns, of course—and there is widespread debate about the balance between private gains, public goods, and planning-induced uncertainties and blight. But if we are to judge by low responses to even the sounder examples of public participation, few people seriously believe that their views can prevail against the twin-headed Leviathan of the local bureaucratic state and the private-property and formerly active public-housebuilding machines. While many schools and colleges continue to neglect the evolution of local plannedscapes the belief will be perpetuated. Classroom imagery has been adopted by Derek Diamond (1978), who has called the outstanding questions of planning the 'three Es'. *Ecology*, the vogue noun of the late 1960s, endures, in spite of Paul Johnson's premature obituary notice (*The Times*, 12 Oct. 1978) in which he opined that the 'ecology panic' could be the death of capitalism. *Energy* is the vogue word of the 1970s and 80s, and if not yet part of the British subconscious, does appear to alarm and anaesthetize Americans in turn. It excites others who foresee a reduced need for daily travel when global telecommunications allow residence to become workplace in the post-industrial, information-processing society. Questions of *equity* will endure. In whose name are planning proposals made, in whose are controls exercised, and for whose benefit are decisions actually taken? And if implemented, what further adjustments in the physical and social environment do they trigger?

The method currently approved in North America for examining the environmental, economic, and social consequences of proposed major developments is environmental impact analysis (EIA). Catlow and

Thirlwall (1977) have reviewed its applicability to the British planning system, and there is now pressure from the EEC for its widespread adoption (see HL 69, session 1980–1 for the report of the Select Committee on the European Communities). Clark *et al.* (1976) have produced a demonstration manual for major industrial projects. EIAs certainly help to augment the traditional developers' questions–is the scheme profitable, legal, and technically possible?–with wider questions including the ecological reversibility of environmental changes (Firey, 1962, was especially percipient about such questions).

The three Es will in part be affected by three Ds: the total level of *demand* in the economy, the changing *desires* within a pluralistic and complex society, and the professional groups who monopolize *design* skills and approve changes in the built environment. These then are some of the influences that will continue to underlie an understanding of the obviously changing, and yet in part consciously preserved, geography of man-made Britain. For the student of planning decisions, explanation lies in a combination of national legislative frameworks and political ideologies, articulated by local actions at the timescale of monthly planning committee meetings.

Further reading

For political parties' views of desirable changes in planning see the May 1979 general election manifestos. Liberal, Labour, and Conservative showed successively paler shades of 'green'. Bi-partisan scrutiny of planning policies is undertaken by the House of Commons Select Committee on the Environment.

Planned environments for anticipated future life-styles may be viewed in occasional planning competitions, exhibitions, projects, and theses. See, for example, 'A third garden city: outline prospectus', *Town and Country Planning* 48 (1979), 227–35, comments by C. Ward in 49 (1980), 160–1, and by S. Lobbenberg in 'Dreamscapes', ibid. 326–37. Novel features incorporated in the thirty-six futuristic houses of Milton Keynes's 'Homeworld 81' exhibition will doubtless become commonplace; those who cannot visit Bradwell Common neighbourhood should see *Architects' Journal*, 29 Apr. 1981, 777–81. *The Southwark site* (GLC, 1980) is the catalogue of fiteen developers' schemes for the 50 ha Surrey Docks site shown in a public exhibition. Lysander Estates' scheme was preferred, but most novel was Tom Hancock's 'earthlife city'. Even if never built according to plan, elements of visionaries' dreams have a habit of materializing later in more humble guises.

The fullest single source on the evolution and present state of the planning process around the world is A. Whittick, ed. (1974) *Encyclopaedia of urban planning* (McGraw-Hill). Studies of environmental impact analysis form a theme issue of *Built Environment* (Vol. 4, No. 2, June 1978).

References

(All books are published in Great Britain unless stated otherwise.)

Acts of Parliament referred to in the text may usually be consulted at larger public libraries; many libraries also subscribe to loose-leaf planning, housing, and land law encyclopaedias that offer an up-to-date explanation of current legislation.

Aldous, T. (1972) *Battle for the environment* (Fontana/Collins).

Ambrose, P. and Colenutt, B. (1975) *The property machine* (Penguin).

Amery, C. and Cruickshank, D. (1975) *The rape of Britain* (Elek).

Anson, B. (1981) *I'll fight you for it: behind the struggle for Covent Garden* (Cape).

Ardill, J. (1974) *The new citizen's guide to town and country planning* (Charles Knight, for TCPA).

Banham, R., Barker, P., Hall, P., and Price, C. (1969) 'Non-plan: an experiment in freedom', *New Society*, 21 Mar. 1969, 435–43.

Barlow, Sir A. M., chm. (1940) *Report of the Royal Commission on the Distribution of the Industrial Population* (Cmd. 6153, HMSO).

Beaver, S. H. (1968) 'Changes in industrial land use, 1930–67', in Institute of British Geographers *Special Publication* 1, 101–9.

Beesley, M. E. and Kettle, P. B. (1979) 'The Leitch committee's recommendations and the management of the road programme', *Regional Studies* 13, 513–29.

Bell, C. and Bell, R. (1969) *City fathers: the early history of town planning in Britain* (Barrie & Rockliff; new edn. Peguin, 1972).

Bell, C. and Newby, H. (1978) 'Community, communion, class and community action: the social sources of the new urban politics', in Herbert, D. T. and Johnston, R. J., eds., *Social areas in cities: processes, patterns and problems* (Wiley), 283–301.

Berry, B. J. L. (1971) 'The geography of the United States in the year 2000', *Trans, Inst. Br. Geogr.* 51, 21–54.

Berthoud, R. (1976) 'Where are London's poor?', *Greater London Intelligence Quarterly* 36, 5–12.

Best, R. H. (1976) 'The extent and growth of urban land', *The Planner* 62, 8–11.

Breach, I. (1978) *Windscale fallout: a primer for the age of nuclear controversy* (Penguin).

Buchanan, C. D., working group chm. (1963) *Traffic in towns: a study of the long-term problems of traffic in urban areas: report of the Steering Group and Working Group appointed by the Minister of Transport* (HMSO).

— (1973) *The state of Britain* (Faber).

Bugler, J. (1978) 'Windscale: a case study in public scrutiny', *New Society*, 27 July 1978, 183–6.

Campbell, R. (1979) 'Population projections: English regions and counties', *Population Trends* 16, 17–21.

Catlow, J. and Thirlwall, C. G. (1977) *Environmental impact analysis* (DoE *Research Report* 11).

Cherry, G. E. (1975) *Environmental planning 1939–1969, Vol. II: National parks and recreation in the countryside* (Peacetime History series, HMSO).

— ed. (1976) *Rural planning problems* (Leonard Hill).

Christensen, T. (1979) *Neighbourhood survival: the struggle for Covent Garden's future* (Prism Press).

Civic Trust (1976) *The local amenity movement* (Civic Trust).

Clark, B. D., Chapman, K., Bisset, R., and Wathern, P. (1976) *Assessment of major industrial applications: a manual* (DoE *Research Report* 13).

Cmd., Cmnd, citations in the text refer to Command (or 'White') Papers in the old and new series, respectively.

Cockburn, C. (1977) *The local state: management of cities and people* (Pluto Press).

Coleman, A. (1969) 'A geographical model for land use analysis', *Geography* 54, 43–55.
— (1977) 'Land use planning: success or failure?', *Architects' Journal*, 19 Jan. 1977, 94–134.
Community Development Project (1977) *The costs of industrial change* (CDP).
Counter Information Services (1978) *The nuclear disaster* (CIS *Anti-Report* 22).
Countryside Commission (1968a) *The coasts of England and Wales: measurements of use, protection and development* (HMSO).
— (1968b) *The planning of the coastline* (HMSO).
— (1969) *The coastal heritage* (HMSO).
— (1979) *11th annual report 1977–78* (HC 111, HMSO).
Countryside Review Committee (1976) *The countryside–problems and policies, a discussion paper* (HMSO).
— (1979) *Conservation and the countryside heritage* (*Topic Paper* 4, HMSO).
Cowan, P., ed. (1973) *The future of planning* (Heinemann).
Cowan, R. (1978) 'Innovations in new towns', *Town and Country Planning* 46, 447–74.
Croall, S. and Sempler, K. (1978) *Nuclear power for beginners* (Beginners Books).
Crosland, A. (1971) *A social democratic Britain* (*Fabian Tract* 404).
Crossman, R. (1975) *Diaries of a cabinet minister, Vol. 1, Minister of Housing, 1964–66* (Hamish Hamilton; condensed edn. in Magnum Books, 1979).
Cullingworth, J. B. (1975) *Environmental planning 1939–1969, Vol. I, Reconstruction and land use planning 1939–1947* (Peacetime History series, HMSO).
— (1979) *Vol. III, New towns* (HMSO).
Damer, S. and Hague, C. (1971) 'Public participation in planning: a review', *Town Planning Review* 42, 217–32;
Davidson, J. and Lloyd, R., eds. (1977) *Conservation and agriculture* (Wiley).
Davidson, J. and Wibberley, G. (1977) *Planning and the rural environment* (Pergamon).
Davies, R. L. (1977) *Marketing geography, with special reference to retailing* (Methuen).
Deakin, N. D. and Ungerson, C. (1977) *Leaving London: planned mobitity and the inner city* (Heinemann).
Dearlove, J. (1979) *The reorganisation of British local government: old orthodoxies and a political perspective* (CUP).
Department of the Environment (1973) 'Making towns better': *Oldham study, Rotherham study, Sunderland study* (HMSO).
— and Welsh Office (1973) *Structure plans: the examination in public* (DoE).
— (1975) *National land use classification*, report of JLA/LAMSACC/SDD/DoE study team (HMSO).
— (1976) *British cities: urban population and employment trends 1951–71* (*Research Report* 10).
— (1977) *Inner area studies: Liverpool, Birmingham and Lambeth. Summaries of the consultants' final reports* (HMSO).
— (1978) *Land availability: a study of land with residential planning permission* (DoE).
Department of Industry (1980) *Guide to regional industrial policy changes, July 1979 to August 1982* (DI).
Department of Trade (1974) *Maplin: review of airport project* (HMSO).
Diamond, D. (1978) Editorial in *Town and Country Planning* 46, 55.
Dobry, G. (1975) *Review of the development control system, final report* (HMSO).
Dower, J. (1945) *National parks in England and Wales* (Cmd. 6628, HMSO).
Draper, P. (1977) *Creation of the D.o.E.* (*Civil Service Studies* 4, HMSO).
Duncan, S. S. (1974) 'Cosmetic planning or social engineering? Improvement grants and improvement areas in Huddersfield', *Area* 6, 259–71.
Eastern Road Construction Unit (1979) *Hackney to M11 Link Road: summary of Joint Working Party report* (ERCU, Bedford).
Economy Group, Development of the Strategic Plan for the South East Team (1976) *Issues report* (DoE).
Eversley, D. (1973) *The planner in society: the changing role of a profession* (Faber).
— (1978) 'Welfare', in Council of Europe, *Population decline in Europe: implications of a declining or stationary population* (Arnold), 115–42.

— and Moody, M. (1976) *The growth of planning research since the early 1960s* (SSRC).

Expenditure Committee of the House of Commons: the work of this select committee and its offshoot Environment Sub-committee is now undertaken by the Select Committee on the Environment constituted in 1979.

Fairbrother, N. (1970) *New lives, new landscape* (Architectural Press; new edn. Penguin, 1972).

Faludi, A., ed. (1973) *A reader in planning theory* (Pergamon).

Firey, W. (1962) *Man, mind, land: a theory of resource appraisal* (Free Press, Glencoe, Illinois).

Flood, M. and Grove-White, R. (1976) *Nuclear prospects: a comment on the individual, the state and nuclear power* (Friends of the Earth in assoc. with CPRE and NCCL).

Flowers, Sir, B., chm. (1976) *Royal Commission on Environmental Pollution, sixth report: nuclear power and the environment* (Cmnd. 6618, HMSO; see also *Government response,* Cmnd. 6820, 1977).

Garner, J. F. *et al.* (1979) 'Policy forum: Skeffington revisited', *Town Planning Review* 50, 412–36.

George-Brown, Lord (1971) *In my way* (Gollancz).

Gilg, A. W. (1979) *Countryside planning: the first three decades 1945–76* (David & Charles, and Methuen).

Gladstone, F. (1976) *The politics of planning* (Temple Smith).

Goodall, B. (1972) *The economics of urban areas* (Pergamon).

Greaster London Council (1979) *1988 Olympic Games: feasibility study* (GLC).

— (1979) *Report from County Hall: London 1977–79* (GLC).

Gregory, R. (1971) *The price of amenity: five studies in conservation and government* (Macmillan).

— (1975) 'The Cow Green reservoir', in Smith, J. R., ed., *The politics of physical resources* (Penguin), 144–201.

Hall, C. (1974) *How to run a pressure group* (Dent/Aldine).

Hall, J. F. (1976) 'Subjective measures of quality of life in Britain 1971 to 1975. Some developments and trends', *Social Trends* 7, 47–60.

Hall, J. M. (1974) 'Forest recreation', in Lavery, P., ed., *Recreational geography* (David & Charles), 145–66.

Hall, P. (1974) 'The containment of urban England', *Geogrl. J.* 140, 386–408 plus discussion to 417.

— ed. (1977) *Europe 2000* (Duckworth).

Hall, P., Gracey, H., Drewett, R., and Thomas, R. (1973) *The containment of urban England: Vol. I, Urban and metropolitan growth processes or megalopolis denied; Vol. II, The planning system: objectives, operations, impacts* (Allen & Unwin).

Hallett, G. (1979) *Urban land economics* (Macmillan).

Hambleton, R. (1978) *Policy planning and local government* (Hutchinson).

Hamnett, C. (1979) 'Area based explanation: a critical appraisal', in Herbert, D. T. and Smith, D. M., eds, *Social problems and the city: geographical perspectives* (OUP), 244–60.

Hampton, W. (1970) *Democracy and community: a study of politics in Sheffield* (OUP).

Hart, D. A. (1976) *Strategic planning in London: the rise and fall of the primary road network* (Pergamon).

Harvey, D. (1973) *Social justice and the city* (Arnold).

— (1976) 'Labor, capital and class struggle around the built environment in advanced capitalist societies', *Politics and Society* 6, 265–95.

HC and HL citations in the text refer to House of Commons and House of Lords papers, which are identified by the serial number from the particular Parliamentary session in which they appeared.

HC *Debates* and HL *Debates* citations in the text refer to the published Parliamentary Debates (Hansard) in the House of Commons and House of Lords.

Hillman, M. and Walley, A. (1972) *Fair play for all* (*PEP Broadsheet* 571).

Hobhouse, Sir A., chm. (1947) *Report of the National Parks Committee* (*England and Wales*) (Cmd. 7121, HMSO).

House, J. W., ed. (1977) *The UK space: resources, environment and the future* (Weidenfeld).

Hunt, Sir J., chm. (1969) *The intermediate areas* (Cmnd. 3998, HMSO).

Inter-departmental Study Group (1971) *Long term population distribution in Great Britain—a study* (HMSO, for DoE).

Kennard, M. F. and Reader, R. A. (1975) 'Cow Green dam and reservoir', *Proceedings Institution of Civil Engineers,* Part I, 58, 147–75.

Kilbrandon, Lord, chm. (1973) *Royal Commission on the Constitution 1969–1973, Vol. I, Report* (Cmnd. 5460, HMSO).

Land Decade Educational Council (1979) *Land-use perspectives* (ed. by L. Fairweather from articles in the *Architects' Journal,* 1976–9) (LDEC).

Lassière, A. (1976) *The environmental evaluation of transport plans* (DoE *Research Report* 8).

Layfield, F., chm. (1976) *Report of the Committee of Inquiry into Local Government Finance* (Cmnd. 6453, HMSO).

Leitch, Sir G., chm. (1977) *Report of the Advisory Committee on Trunk Road Assessment* (HMSO, for DTp).

Lloyd, D., gen. ed. (1976) *Save the City: a conservation study of the City of London* (Society for the Protection of Ancient Buildings, and others).

Local Government Training Board (1977) *Development control case studies, No. 1: Mrs Warren's cloakroom* (part of 6 case studies plus tutor's manual) (LGTB, Luton).

MacEwan, M., ed (1976) *Future landscapes* (Chatto & Windus).

Mackintosh, J. P. (1968) *The devolution of power* (Penguin).

Marshall, Sir F. (1978) *The Marshall Inquiry on Greater London: report to the Greater London Council by Sir Frank Marshall* (GLC).

Massey, D. and Catalano, A. (1978) *Capital and land: landowership by capital in Great Britain* (Arnold).

Meyerson, M. and Banfield, E. C. (1955) *Politics, planning and the public interest: the case of public housing in Chicago* (Free Press of Glencoe, Illinois).

Milton Keynes Development Corporation (1970) *The plan for Milton Keynes,* Vol. I (principal consultants: Llewelyn-Davies, Weeks, Forestier-Walker, and Bor) (MKDC).

Ministry of Housing and Local Government (1964) *The South East study, 1961–1981* (HMSO).

— (1966) *The Deeplish study: improvement possibilities in a district of Rochdale* (HMSO).

— (1970) *Development plans—a manual on form and content* (HMSO).

Morrison, B. (1978) 'The progress of structure planning in England and Wales', *Built Environment* 4, 328–31.

National Parks Commission (1967–8) 9 regional volumes for England and Wales, each entitled *The coasts of . . .* (regional name) (HMSO).

Natural Environment Research Council (1977) *A nature conservation review: the selection of biological sites of national importance to nature conservation in Britain* (2 vols.) (CUP for NCC/NERC).

— (1978) *Land use mapping by local authorities in Britain* (a report commissioned by the DoE, prepared by the Experimental Cartography Unit) (Architectural Press).

Nature Conservancy Council (1977) *Nature conservation and agriculture: appraisal and proposals* (NCC).

Newman, O. (1976) *Defensible space: people and design in the violent city* (Architectural Press).

North Hertfordshire District Council (1978) *Letchworth Garden City 1903–1978, a commemorative exhibition: catalogue of exhibits* (NHDC); see also Garden Cities issue of *Vole,* Vol. 2, No. 6, March 1979.

Parker, R. J. (1978) *Windscale inquiry: report by the Hon. Mr Justice Parker, Vol. I, Report and Annexes 3–5* (HMSO).

Parry, M. L. (1977) *Mapping moorland change: a framework for land use de*
in the Peak District (Peak District National Park; quoted in *Landsc*
4 (1979), 24–5).

Pearce, D., Edwards, L., and Bennett, G. (1979) *Decision mak*
futures: case study of the Windscale inquiry (Macmillan).

Perman, D. (1973) *Cublington: a blueprint for resistance* (Bodley Hea

Pigott, C. D. (1956) 'The vegetation of Upper Teesdale in the Nort
Journal of Ecology 44, 545–86.

Planning Advisory Group (1965) *Report, The future of development plans* (HMSO, for MHLG).
Plowden, Lady, chm. (1967) *Children and their primary schools, report of the Central Advisory Council for Education (England)* (HMSO).
Porchester, Lord (1977) *Report, A study of Exmoor* (HMSO, for DoE and MAFF).
Ratcliffe, J. (1976) *Land policy: an exploration of the nature of land in society* (Hutchinson).
Redcliffe-Maud, Lord, chm. (1969) *Royal Commission on Local Government in England 1966–1969, Vol. I, Report* (Cmnd. 4040, HMSO).
Reith, Lord, chm. (1946) *New Towns Committee: final report* (Cmd. 6876, HMSO).
Robbins, Lord, chm. (1963) *Report of the Committee on Higher Education* (Cmnd. 2154, HMSO).
Roskill, E., chm. (1971) *Report of the Commission on the Third London Airport* (HMSO).
Royal Town Planning Institute (1976) *Planning and the future* (RTPI).
Sandford, Revd Lord, chm. (1974) *Report of the National Park Policies Review Committee* (HMSO, for DoE).
Saunders, P. (1979) *Urban politics: a sociological interpretation* (Hutchinson; new edn. Penguin, 1980).
Scott, Lord Justice, chm. (1942) *Report of the Committee on Land Utilisation in Rural Areas* (Cmd. 6378, HMSO).
Sharp, E. (1969) *The Ministry of Housing and Local Government* (Allen & Unwin).
Sheail, J. (1976) *Nature in trust: the history of conservation in Britain* (Blackie).
Skeffington, A. M., chm. (1969) *People and planning: report of the Committee on Public Participation in Planning* (HMSO, for DoE/SDD/WO).
Social Science Research Council (1976) *Research priorities of the SSRC Planning Committee* (SSRC Planning Committee Paper No. 1).
— (1980) *The inner city in context* (series of 11 reports which will form the basis of a programme of new research).
Statham. D. (1972) 'Natural resources in the uplands: capability analysis in the North York Moors', *Journal of the Royal Town Planning Institute* 58, 468–78.
Strutt, Sir N., chm. (1978) *Agriculture and the countryside, report of the Advisory Council for Agriculture and Horticulture* (MAFF).
Taylor, J. L. (1971) *Instructional planning systems* (CUP).
Tetlow, J. and Goss, A. (1968) *Homes, towns and traffic* (2nd edn., Faber).
Thomas, D. (1970) *London's green belt* (Faber).
Thomson, J. M. (1969) *Motorways in London* (Duckworth, for LATA).
Town and Country Planning Association (1978) *Planning and plutonium: evidence of the TCPA to the public inquiry into an oxide re-processing plant at Windscale* (TCPA).
Towsend, P. (1976) 'Area deprivation studies', *New Statesman*, 6 Aug. 1976, 168–71.
Tyme, J. (1978) *Motorways versus democracy: public inquiries into road proposals and their political significance* (Macmillan).
Uthwatt, Lord Justice, chm. (1942) *Report of the Expert Committee on Compensation and Betterment* (Cmd. 6386, HMSO).
Ward, C. (1979) *The child in the city* (Peguin).
Warren, K. (1978) 'Issues over resources', in Davies, R. and Hall, P., ed., *Issues in urban society* (Peguin), 53–83.
Wates, N. (1976) *The battle for Tolmers Square* (Routledge).
Wells, H. G. (1903) *Mankind in the making* (Chapman & Hall).
Westmacott, R. and Worthington, T. (1974) *New agricultural landscapes* (Countryside Commission CCP 76; see also *Discussion Paper* 76A (1974) and *New agricultural landscapes–issues, objectives and action*, CCP 102 (1977)).
Willatts, E. C. (1962) 'Post-war developments: the location of major projects in England and Wales', *Chartered Surveyor* 94, 356–63 and 436–8.
— (1971) 'Planning and geography in the last three decades', *Geogrl. J.* 137, 311–30 plus discussion to 338.
Wraith, R. E. and Lamb G. B. (1971) *Public inquiries as an instrument of government* (Allen & Unwin).
Young, K. and Kramer, J. (1978) *Strategy and conflict in metropolitan housing: suburbia versus the Greater London Council 1965–75* (Heinemann).